Garth Hewitt is an international troubadour for the Anglican Communion. I know of many men and women, particularly in the Middle East, who have been profoundly moved and inspired by his songs. He is one of those rare people who feeds on hope; this book is a clear testimony to both his Christian faith and his artistry.

+ Richard Chartres, Bishop of London

Garth Hewitt is Regional Co-ordinator for London and the South East for Christian Aid. He is also Guild Vicar of All Hallows on the Wall and Director of the Amos Trust. All Hallows on the Wall is home to Christian Aid's London and South East Team and the Amos Trust and the church is developing as a resource centre for issues of justice, peace and development.

Garth is well known as a singer and songwriter, having released nearly thirty albums. For twenty-five years he was on the board of the Greenbelt Festivals as one of those who shaped its direction.

His last book, 'Pilgrims and Peacemakers—a journey towards Jerusalem', was also published by The Bible Reading Fellowship.

Contact address for Garth, Christian Aid London & South East or the Amos Trust: All Hallows on the Wall, 83 London Wall, London EC2M 5ND. Fax 0171-588 2663 and e-mail: amos_trust@compurserve.com

D1150776

Text copyright © Garth Hewitt 1999
The author asserts the moral right to be
identified as the author of this work

Published by
The Bible Reading Fellowship
Peter's Way, Sandy Lane West
Oxford OX4 5HG
ISBN 1 84101 041 3

First published 1999
1 3 5 7 9 10 8 6 4 2 0

Acknowledgments
Unless otherwise stated, scripture quotations are taken from
The New Revised Standard Version of the Bible, Anglicized
Edition, copyright © 1989, 1995 by the Division of Christian
Education of the National Council of the Churches of Christ
in the USA, and are used by permission. All rights reserved.

New English Bible with the Apocrypha: Oxford Study Edition
copyright © 1976 by Oxford University Press, Inc.

A catalogue record for this book is available
from the British Library

Printed and bound in Great Britain by
Caledonian Book Manufacturing International, Glasgow

A Candle of Hope

A journey through Advent,
Christmas and the New Year
to Bethlehem

GARTH HEWITT

PREFACE

Advent provides the Christian community with a new beginning, and new beginnings provide new opportunities for people. Since all of us are on a journey in life, it is good to continue to look for new opportunities and fresh starts. In thinking about the future as we draw near to the year of jubilee and to the new millennium, we hope and pray that there will be a new beginning for the human race at large and, in particular, for the people in the Middle East. It is here that the legacy of our past has been one of so much suffering. Let us pray that the mistrust among the nations that make up the Middle East, be they Christians, Jews or Muslims, be forgotten, and that the three faiths could join hands to protect what is left of the beauty of that area which God has chosen and made so special and which has become so central in the faith of the three monotheistic communities. Let all of us join hands to remedy the past and help shape the future.

While Advent takes the thoughts of people to the second coming of Christ, some evangelicals continue to hope and pray that catastrophic happenings will occur in the Middle East to hasten this second coming. Meanwhile we continue to pray and work for a more beautiful Middle East, so that when Jesus comes back in his second coming, he will have a joyful community welcoming him rather than people with tears, weeping over the many killed, especially with weapons of mass destruction.

So Advent is a time when we look back to the past and have the need to repent of all the things that have been done that have caused unrest and distorted the image of God in the lives of all people created in his image. At the same time, Advent places our feet on a road of fresh hope for a new age and a new era with all the challenges and opportunities that this brings. The Christian community is called to be a community that plants hope in hopeless situations, a community that shares life, even in the midst of death. Garth's book is called *A Candle Of Hope*—in the Middle East situation, what would bring hope is peace with justice, an end to the conflict, and an end to the enmity, and an end to hostility. To put an end to enmity, we do not need to kill the enemy; we want to kill the enmity and to help the enemy to become the friend.

Our hope is that the Palestinians will be guaranteed a place under the sun and will be allowed to live in an independent homeland, a state of their own on Palestinian soil, side by side with Israel, where the two could become the hope of the hopeless in a world where there is a lot of pain and much conflict.

The Church, too, must be a place of hope, for the Church cannot give what it lacks. Only a community that has peace can share peace with others. A community that is hopeful can lead people into believing in a hopeful situation. You cannot give what you don't have.

I am delighted to write this preface for my friend and brother, Garth. I've already said of his songs that they are so inspiring, so informative, so balanced and so truthful, and that they have told the story of our pain. Now, on this journey, he encourages us to see the significance of the birth of Jesus in Bethlehem, the significance of 'God with us', walking beside us. He refuses just to pietize the gospel, and says, 'If it is real, it must work today in the pain and struggle for justice and peace between Palestinian and Jew.'

I hope many will enter the new millennium and succeeding years walking this journey and meeting the 'living stones' of the Holy Land in the book *A Candle Of Hope*. Then, as a result of this, come and visit us in this land that we long to make holy—we will give you a wonderful welcome... but do not come and pass us by. We need your visits, your support, your fellowship and your prayers. Together let us light candles that bring true hope for a new millennium.

Riah Hanna Abu El-Assal, Anglican Bishop in Jerusalem
Jerusalem, August 1998

Contents

INTRODUCTION

BETHLEHEM—A CANDLE OF HOPE

Many eyes turn to Bethlehem at the millennium—certainly Christian eyes, as we remember the birth of Jesus in a stable and the haunting promise of peace from the angels. After *Pilgrims and Peacemakers—A Journey Towards Jerusalem* I am delighted now to do a second journey, this time to Bethlehem. In *Pilgrims and Peacemakers*, the gospel set the journey and we followed Jesus. In this book, the birthplace itself will be at the centre. We will move out from this remarkable Palestinian town on journeys of discovery in biblical history, theology, and in terms of the modern-day Palestinian and Israeli people, their own history so starkly and savagely carved into the hillsides of the Shepherds' Fields round Bethlehem.

Some of the same characters will reappear in this book telling further stories but there are also new ones. Christian, Muslim and Jew will tell their tales and talk of hope. I have visited nearly every year, once or twice, for the last ten years, but the key time for collecting this material was February 1998—expecting another Gulf war and feeling the pain of derailed peace talks, I have never known such pain or despair. For some, the flicker of hope had gone out altogether. For others, they clung to it, often because of a gospel of hope which started in Bethlehem—against all the odds.

Because even 'a week in politics is a long time' the political situation may well have changed by the time this book is read—I hope so, and hope that the journey to peace and justice will have progressed significantly.

In *A Candle of Hope*, the journey follows the pattern of Advent to Christmas—indeed, the three Christmases celebrated in the Holy Land. Then to the New Year and on to Epiphany, lighting candles as we go. On our journey, once again our hosts will be the Palestinian church that has witnessed in this part of the world for centuries and continues its witness today, even though it is a shrinking population. We will also hear the voices of peacemakers amongst the Jewish and Muslim communities. I hope the book will encourage you to visit the Holy Land and to use this book as you travel, as has happened with

Pilgrims and Peacemakers. But, as before, I would say, don't visit the Holy Land unless you meet with the 'living stones'—the local Christian community, which is predominantly a Palestinian one. We must not visit their world and pass by on the other side. We must allow them to be our hosts, our guides. We must listen to them and learn from them.

Advent is a wonderful time of year, a time of expectancy and hope, a time of lighting candles and opening advent calendars, a time when we wait for light to come out of the darkness again, a time when we are reminded of the importance of light coming into our world in the birth of Jesus at Bethlehem two thousand years ago.

Evidently, just before the turn of the last millennium, there was a rise of religious fervour, fundamentalism and apocalyptic interest that was to result, eighty or ninety years later, in the first Crusade. The horror of the Crusades is a terrible part of Christian history. Jews were killed in Europe as Christians headed down to 'liberate' the Holy Land from the Muslim. Even Christians were killed in the Holy Land as the crusaders didn't even realize that there were Christian villages. Insensitivity, arrogance of religion, colonialism and aggression all add up to a very unpleasant story. The Jewish theologian, Marc Ellis, warns of what he calls the 'Constantinian' danger for any religion. In other words, what happened to Christianity when Constantine made it the official religion for the Roman Empire is a danger for the message of faith. Marc suggests that it turns religion into being a religion of 'empire' rather than a religion of 'community'. Consequently dominance and aggression, and maybe grandeur, can become its mark rather than the simplicity, the community values and the serving nature which are the alternative. Marc warns each religion that this can happen, just as it did for Christians in the time of Constantine.

Finally, some thanks are due—first to the many people I interviewed. I hope I have faithfully reflected what they said. I am grateful for people being so honest and inspired when my Dictaphone was thrust in front of them. Special thanks to Bishop Riah and Suad and their family, who have been so hospitable and helpful and such good friends, and thanks to Riah for the preface. Also very grateful thanks to Gill King, who typed the whole book for me—corrections and all. Gill did this for *Pilgrims and Peacemakers* and foolishly thought I would make the Advent book shorter and so agreed to do it! Thank you so much, it would not have happened without you. Much of the information for this book was collected in February 1998 and for part of the time I was touring around with a group of young people from the Amos Collective. Many thanks to them and to Beki Bateson of the Amos Trust for finishing off some of the interviews, and to Stephen Sizer, friend and Amos Trustee and key supporter on my journeys there. I promised the Amos Collective a mention. They were Jonny Baker, Katie Goulbourn, Michael Bishop, Paul Cleever-Thorpe, Ian Haffenden, Caty Pannell, Abi Rushton, Naomi Russell and Richard and Ann Wise. They were an inspiring group with which to travel. Thanks also to Mary Lou Smith from North Carolina who was over for the Sabeel Conference in Bethlehem, who also took time out to guide me round various projects and people. Thanks also to all at Christian Aid and especially to Jean and the London and South East team, and the Community Fundraising Unit and to Tim Moulds for considerable patience! Also to Clare at Amos. Finally thanks to Gill, who has done many of my Holy Land journeys with me, and also to the family, Tom, Ben, Abi and Joe. They are a constant inspiration to me.

Garth Hewitt
September 1998

ADVENT 1

Watching and Waiting

Advent—How It Began

Nobody knows exactly how Advent started but the custom is very ancient. In his History of the Franks, *Saint Gregory of Tours wrote that one of his predecessors, Saint Perpetuus, who held the See around 480, decreed a fast three times a week from the feast of Saint Martin, 11 November, until Christmas. In 567, the second Council of Tours enjoined monks to fast from the beginning of December until Christmas. This penance was soon extended to the laity and was pushed back to begin on Saint Martin's Day. This forty-five day Advent was nicknamed 'Saint Martin's Lent'. From France the practice of doing penance during Advent spread to England, as is noted in Venerable Bede's* History.

From Hubert Dunphy, *Advent*, published by Liturgy Training Publications

This is what Advent is

Advent should admonish us to discover
In each brother or sister that we greet,
In each friend whose hand we shake,
In each beggar who asks for bread,
In each worker who wants to use the right to join a union,
In each peasant who looks for work in the coffee groves,
The face of Christ.

Then it would not be possible to rob them,
To cheat them,
To deny them their rights.

They are Christ,
And whatever is done to them
Christ will take as done to him.

That is what Advent is:
Christ living among us.

Oscar Romero (1917–80)

No more gloom

Isaiah 9:2–7

The people who walked in darkness have seen a great light; those who lived in a land of deep darkness—on them light has shined... The yoke of their burden, and... the rod of their oppressor, you have broken as on the day of Midian. For all the boots of the tramping warriors and all the garments rolled in blood shall be burned as fuel for the fire. For a child has been born for us, a son given to us; authority rests upon his shoulders; and he is named Wonderful Counsellor, Mighty God... Prince of Peace. His authority shall grow continually, and there shall be endless peace for the throne of David and his kingdom. He will establish and uphold it with justice and with righteousness from this time onward and for evermore.

About 750 years before the birth of Jesus Christ, Isaiah the prophet was speaking. He carried out his ministry close to Jerusalem. Not much is known about him but he was clearly a person with great literary abilities, as well as a deep concern about social justice and the character of God. This is a good passage with which to start our Advent journey, which will end up just a few miles away down the road in Bethlehem. It's a good place to start because these remarkable words from the Hebrew scriptures are seen by Christians as a reflection of the character of the one who will come from 'Galilee of the nations'—issuing a Nazareth mandate—and bring light into a dark world. It reminds us, as we watch and wait, that we must never forget that a light has come into the world and that the values of this child who is born for us will bring justice and peace and the reign of a very different kingdom. People will rejoice because liberation will follow.

Religion has a chequered history and my journeys to the Middle East have reminded me of this. So, too, have my journeys to Northern Ireland and to Croatia and the Bosnian refugees; and one of the key tests to see whether we are following the right way is to ask, 'Does this liberate or oppress?' This can be true in more local and personal ways. Powerful charismatic leaders can manipulate people and the result can be oppression rather than liberation, but the one who came from 'Galilee of the nations' said he had come to bring 'good news for the poor' and 'to set free the oppressed'. An exciting aspect of verse 5 is the reminder that the blood and the violence will end—'the boots of the tramping warriors and all the garments rolled in blood shall be burned as fuel for the fire'. The ways of the Prince of Peace will reject the ways of dominance, violence, aggression and 'empire', and instead be the ways of community and hope that will increase people's joy.

In a curious way, Advent has the imagery of childbirth, the pregnant expectancy of the birth of hope, and it's not without its birth pangs. There are some words from one of the Dead Sea Scrolls that reflect this (Hymn column 3.4.12, 18).

Like a woman in travail
With her firstborn child,
Upon whose belly pangs have come
And grievous pains,
Filling with anguish her child-bearing crucible.

For the children have come to the throes of death,
And she labours in her pains who bears a man.
For amid the throes of Death
She shall bring forth a man-child,
And amid the pains of Hell
There shall spring from her child-bearing crucible,

A Marvellous Mighty Counsellor
And a man shall be delivered out of the throes.

This passage has an echo of the words from the prophet Isaiah, and contains the thought that 'the Wonderful Counsellor, Mighty God, Prince of Peace' comes after the anguish.

J. Massyngbaerde Ford comments on these words from the Dead Sea Scrolls in her book, *Days Of The Spirit* (Liturgical Press, 1994) and says, 'Through awesome travail the community writhes in the throes of childbirth to bring forth the Son of justice who alone can bring security. There is no security unless it is based on justice.'

PRAYER

All praise and thanks to you, God of the starry night, for the light of Christ, which blazes forth and scatters our darkness. In this holy season, your people turn their faces to the coming of your justice and peace. Amid the approaching shades and chill of earth, we await the return of the Saviour whose coming is our hope and your promise. Your power is kindled so that we might not be tempted to despair. All praise and thanks be yours through Jesus Christ and the Holy Spirit for ever and ever. Amen

From *Prayers for Dawn and Dusk* by Edward F. Gabriele, St Mary's Press, 1992

TO DO

Write down the name of somebody whose name you will mention at the lighting of the candle later this week—someone who groans in pain or suffering at this time, someone who needs your prayers.

MONDAY OF WEEK 1

KEEP AWAKE

MATTHEW 25:1–13

Then the kingdom of heaven will be like this. Ten bridesmaids took their lamps and went to meet the bridegroom. Five of them were foolish, and five were wise. When the foolish took their lamps, they took no oil with them; but the wise took flasks of oil with their lamps… But at midnight there was a shout, 'Look! Here is the bridegroom! Come out to meet him.' Then all those bridesmaids got up and trimmed their lamps. The foolish said to the wise, 'Give us some of your oil, for our lamps are going out.' But the wise replied, 'No! there will not be enough for you and for us; you had better go to the dealers and buy some for yourselves.' And while they went to buy it, the bridegroom came, and those who were ready went with him into the wedding banquet; and the door was shut. Later the other bridesmaids came also, saying, 'Lord, lord, open to us.' But he replied, 'Truly I tell you, I do not know you.' Keep awake therefore, for you know neither the day nor the hour.

This curious story of ten bridesmaids with no mention of a bride is to warn us of the danger of our love growing cold, of failing to keep awake in terms of witnessing to the values of God's reign. The bridegroom is the 'God of surprises' whom we find in unexpected places and coming at unexpected times. This parable reminds us to be alert to the opportunities that present themselves and to be aware of what is happening around us so that we can be part of a community involved in the struggle for what is right.

Louise and Connor Taaffe, coming out of their local Catholic church in Eltham, cannot have expected to stumble across the badly wounded body of Stephen Lawrence. Unprepared as they must have been in one sense, in another sense they were prepared, and Louise said some remarkable words to him as he lay dying: 'You are loved, you are loved.'

Our lives so far should prepare us to be ready when the moment comes. Rosa Parks, as she sat on the bus on 1 December 1955 in Montgomery, Alabama, refused to give up her seat. It was a significant act in the struggle for the values of the kingdom of God and it was her own Christian faith and understanding of the Bible that led her to this point.

From my upbringing and the Bible, I learned people should stand up for their rights, just as the children of Israel stood up to Pharaoh. When I reflect on conditions in the south, I recall that people had become worn out from being humiliated. They were sick of accepting the racial segregation that seemed to be worsening each day. Someone had to take that first step. In that moment on the bus, I decided to resist and take the consequences. It was worth it. I'm glad to know that this and many other incidents have brought change.
Rosa Parks, from *Quiet Strength*, Zondervan, 1994

Sometimes all our lives seem to lead up to one point and if we've stayed awake and alert and allowed ourselves to be nurtured on the values of the gospel, we are ready when the opportunity is presented to act like the Taaffes or Rosa Parks.

If you're familiar with Polish composer Gorecki's Third Symphony, you will know that it starts with a low hum which is almost inaudible at first but gradually builds. It takes about twelve minutes before there seems to be any further development, but all the time there is this sense of expectancy and building excitement and something coming. So it is with Advent. It is a low hum which will end in an explosion of light and hope. During this low hum, it is a time for us to review, to look around us, and to think how far we have come from the values of God's reign. As one of the two times of penance in the church's year, it is a time for taking stock, a time for looking round God's world and reviewing what's happening.

As we go through this journey of Advent together and light candles at the end of each week, let us light them for those situations that come up in our review. They could be for people we know, they could be for communities around the world that we should have been praying for and that we may have forgotten. The lighting of the candle might prompt us to write a letter, or to act, or to build further links. Into each of these situations we will be praying, 'Come, Lord Jesus, make a difference, come with your values, come with your reign, come with your compassion, come with your justice, come with your humanity, and make me human, and make me just, and make me loving.'

PRAYER
Lord, may we keep awake to the opportunities you present today. May we be sensitive to the promptings of your Spirit so that when you come, in whatever guise, bringing the opportunity to reflect the values of your reign, we are ready and sensitive because we have been watching and waiting and have been prepared. Amen

TO THINK ABOUT
Is there any situation which we think we should have spoken up about or done something about, that we've ignored? If so, write it down and work out a plan to do something if it is still possible and, if not, make it the spur to being alert next time we are challenged in this way.

HEBRON

Hebron is the oldest continuously occupied unwalled city in the world. It's not far from Bethlehem, past the Dheisheh refugee camp and then a few miles south of Bethlehem, past vineyards and hills and the Israeli settlements on the hilltops, and then into Hebron itself. Hebron is known as Khalil al-Rahman in Arabic. It's regarded as holy by Muslims, Jews and Christians alike because the patriarch Abraham is considered to be buried here. But here also is the sharp end of Israeli occupation as Jewish settlements, built on confiscated Palestinian land, surround the city, and extremist religious settlers have taken over buildings in an area right at the centre of the city over the market. Their occupation is aggressive and unpleasant and the homes of people who live nearby and have lived there with their families for years are extremely vulnerable. Army vehicles surround them on all sides but, nevertheless, you get a strong welcome from the local community.

Hebron was inhabited by Canaanites as early as 2000 BC, though according to Muslim tradition it dates from the beginning of time. Adam and Eve are supposed to have lived here after they were expelled from the Garden of Eden, which may well explain why there is a footprint of Adam in the Mosque of Abraham! The city was well established by the time Abraham and Sarah came here and pitched their tents by the oaks of Mamre. When Moses sent spies to view the land, it was to Hebron they came, and they returned with tales of a land flowing with milk and honey.

The Harem al-Khalil, or the Tomb of the Patriarchs, is obviously the central site in Hebron. It encloses the cave of Makhpela. The walls were constructed by Herod the Great and then there has been additional crusader and Mamluk work on it, making it most impressive. Here, mosque and synagogue are side by side. It was here on 25 February 1994 during Friday prayers that Baruch Goldstein came and massacred twenty-nine Palestinians. One can still see the bullet holes in the walls of the mosque. So Hebron not only has profoundly ancient history, it has deep scars of recent history.

Hebron was the capital city for David when he was king of Judah, before he moved to Jerusalem and reigned over all of Israel and Judah.

In 2 Samuel 2, we discover that God told him to go to Hebron and make it his capital city, and he ruled there for seven years and six months. He was anointed in Hebron as king of Judah, and then later they came and anointed him in Hebron as king of Israel. There was civil war while David was in Hebron, though he soon got the upper hand. 2 Samuel 3 points out that he fathered six sons in Hebron, though all apparently by different mothers. One of these sons was Absalom. Joab, one of David's leaders, killed Abner in the gateway of Hebron. In 1 Samuel 4, the head of Ishbosheth was brought to David in Hebron and he killed those who brought it and put their bodies by the pool of Hebron.

TUESDAY OF WEEK 1

From Iraq to Hebron

GENESIS 12:1–2, 4
Now the Lord said to Abram, 'Go from your country and your kindred and your father's house to the land that I will show you. I will make of you a great nation, and I will bless you, and make your name great, so that you will be a blessing... So Abram went, as the Lord had told him.

These words conceal an extremely long journey that had started long before the words that begin today's reading were spoken. In the previous chapter we discover that Abram was in Ur of the Chaldeans, in what is today's southern Iraq, and was then in Babylon. From there he moved with his family to Haran in northern Syria (then Assyria) and it was there that God told Abram to move south. Abram does this by first going close to modern-day Ramallah, then called Bethel, and then journeying down to the Negev. Because of famine he heads on to Egypt, but in the end is thrown out of Egypt by Pharaoh, having tried to pass his wife off as his sister. He goes back again to Bethel, where there is an argument between Abram's herders and Lot's, and so they divide the land: Lot goes into the area of the plains of Jordan and Abram heads for Hebron.

God has promised to make a great nation of Abram, but now at a very old age he and Sarai have no children, and so Abram sleeps with Hagar, his slave girl, and she gives birth to Ishmael. God renews the covenant with Abram and now calls him Abraham, which in Hebrew is a derivation meaning 'father of a multitude'.

In the Bible story (Genesis 12 through to 17), Abraham and Sarah have made their journey from Iraq, eventually arriving at Hebron. In the present day you can see another group who have made long journeys, largely from North America, who are very visible in Hebron, wearing red hats. They are the Christian Peacemaker Team. They are made up of Mennonites, Brethren and Quakers, who literally stand between the Israeli army and the local indigenous Palestinians, trying to defend them and hear their stories and report their stories to a wider world. They risk their lives daily and would have sympathy with Gandhi's comment, 'Just as one must learn the art of killing in the training for violence, so one must learn the art of dying in the training for non-violence.'

When I first met them, they were doing a fast for seven hundred hours because seven hundred homes were due to be demolished for expanded settlements and roads to these settlements. I was fascinated by the reaction of the local Muslim community. They have enormous affection for the Peacemakers and in some ways view them as 'crazy'! Of course they are—they are fools for Christ's sake. But as I saw the local community bringing them gifts, I also noted that they brought stones, stones from demolished homes to put beside them, like icons of the suffering and the pain that they were experiencing. The local community realized that these people had come on a long journey, from miles away, to stand beside them in their struggle for justice, and they also recognized that they were driven by their understanding of the character of God. On a cold morning we shivered beside the Christian Peacemaker Team and we sang together, joining in a song which is a prayer for peace, *Ten Measures of Beauty*. As we read the words from Isaiah 58 on the kind of fasting that is required from the people of God—a fasting that does not ignore the plight of the poor and the oppressed—the gospel became tangible for me as I prayed with these Peacemakers.

Later we walked round Hebron and visited homes together and I saw that this was a serving group, who were willing to take up their cross daily, regardless of what might happen to themselves. They have received threats to their lives from an extremist Jewish group. They were warned to get out or they would be killed, and accused of smuggling weapons. They told me that threats of death are not a problem to them, because if those threatening them knew their history, they would realize that members of their community have often been killed because of their commitment to non-violence and to the ways of peace.

PRAYER
May our journeying lead us to worthwhile acts where we stand beside those who watch and wait and pray for justice to be done. Amen

PEACEMAKING IN HEBRON

Mark Frey is one of the Christian Peacemakers. He comes from Newton, Kansas, and is a Mennonite by background. He and Diane Roe, who is a United Methodist, have been my hosts, showing me round their work and introducing me to people in Hebron. Talking of why they are there, Mark Frey says:

One of the key events was a speech in 1994 by Ron Sider, where he challenged us that we need to recognize the ways in which we have diminished Jesus' call to be peacemakers. We need to embrace a full biblical understanding of peacemaking, understood as right relationships between people and other people, between ourselves and God, and between ourselves and the environment. He also challenged us that we need to be willing to die—he called for active peacemakers who were willing to take personal risk, to put their lives on the line in much the same way that soldiers do when they make war. He said that until we are ready to make that kind of commitment, we really have no right to criticize militaristic structures. We've been in Hebron for two and a half years, at the invitation of the Hebron municipality. We will go places only after an official invitation is issued by somebody on the ground. In this case it was the mayor. We recognize that sometimes having international eyes, international presence, can keep violent situations from escalating or can deter some violence. But we're not restricted to just observation. We ask questions like, how can we intervene in situations to stop the violence? Sometimes that's possible, and a lot of times it isn't. For example, if we see a soldier beating someone, we will, at the very minimum, go and confront him verbally, and ask, 'What are you doing?' Often that's enough to stop the physical violence from happening. We are willing to consider taking some personal risk in order to deflect or deter violence.

WEDNESDAY OF WEEK 1

THE THREE VISITORS

GENESIS 18:1–5, 7–8

The Lord appeared to Abraham by the oaks of Mamre, as he sat at the entrance of his tent in the heat of the day. He looked up and saw three men standing near him. When he saw them, he ran from the tent entrance to meet them, and bowed down to the ground. He said, 'My lord, if I find favour with you, do not pass by your servant. Let a little water be brought, and wash your feet, and rest yourselves under the tree. Let me bring a little bread, that you may refresh yourselves, and after that you may pass on—since you have come to your servant.' So they said, 'Do as you have said.' … Abraham ran to the herd, and took a calf, tender and good, and gave it to the servant, who hastened to prepare it. Then he took curds and milk and the calf that he had prepared, and set it before them; and he stood by them under the tree while they ate.

What a fascinating and mysterious passage. The first verse talks of the Lord, or Yahweh, appearing to Abraham through these three men who are seen as messengers or angels of God. This passage has often been seen as a reflection of the Trinity, and Rublev's famous icon of that name features these three angels or guests sitting under the tree at Mamre. Abraham certainly treats them with enormous respect and shows typical Middle Eastern hospitality and stands there as they eat. After this (18:9–13), they ask about Sarah, and say that she will have a son. She laughs, because she is well past the age of child-bearing. Yahweh comes back into the story and asks why Sarah laughed. Two

22

or three chapters later we discover that Sarah has become pregnant, and she gives birth to a son whom she calls Isaac, which means 'he laughs'. Sarah plays on that name when she says, 'God has brought laughter for me; everyone who hears will laugh with me' (21:6).

Sarah's joy, though, is soon tempered with jealousy and she insists that Hagar and Ishmael be sent away, a fact which is very distressing to Abraham. However, God encourages him by saying, 'As for the son of the slave woman, I will make a nation of him also, because he is your offspring.' This reflects the promise which was made to Abraham when Yahweh had made a covenant with him saying, 'To your descendants I give this land, from the river of Egypt to the great river, the river Euphrates' (15:18). From Abraham, it appears, there are to be two great nations, and it's to Ishmael that the Arab world trace their roots. When Hagar and Ishmael run out of water in the desert, an angel of God calls to Hagar and reminds her that God is going to make a great nation of her son, and her eyes are opened and she sees a well of water. So there are promises to make great nations of Isaac and Ishmael, and God's promise to give them the land, but this is tempered by the fact that in Leviticus 25:23 God makes it very clear that 'the land is mine; with me you are but aliens and tenants'. Consequently, in that remarkable chapter of jubilee, God gives principles as to how people are to be treated on the land and in the community.

The Orthodox Church sees the concept of Trinity as a reminder that in God there is community, and if you have a copy of Rublev's icon, it's good to sit and meditate on what it means to be community. We don't have to stand at a distance under the trees as Abraham did, but are called to share in the community meal—the communion—which reminds us of the family we are to be and the hospitality, the generosity, the compassion and the justice we should espouse.

PRAYER
Blessed are you, Lord our God, King of the universe, eternal creator of light and darkness. In this season of Advent, when the sun's light is swallowed up by the growing darkness of the night, you renew your promise to reveal among us the splendour of your glory, made flesh and visible to us in Jesus Christ your Son. Through the prophets you teach us to hope for his reign of peace. Through the outpouring of his Spirit, you

open our blindness to the glory of his presence. Strengthen us in our weakness; support us in our stumbling efforts to do your will, and free our tongues to sing your praise. For to you all honour and blessing are due, now and for ever. Amen

From *Praise God in Song*, © GIA Publications Inc.

MEDITATION: HAGAR—AN ICON

You see them everywhere, the Hagars of the world. They are the homeless women of every city round the globe, left with children that someone wanted once but have no use for now... Hagar becomes a light in the darkness, a holy one of God, an icon in the midst of idols. It is in Hagar that the rest of us see the power of dependence on God.

God makes a promise to Hagar as well as to Sarah and Abraham, that the child born to her will also have a birthright, will also be a leader of the nation. On Hagar, too, in other words, lies the burden of the future of the world. In God's promise to Hagar, the poor see that the globe is not simply in the hands of the few who control its resources and command its wealth and consort with its beautiful people. The fate of the world is weighed in the balance between rich and poor; between the Hagars and the Sarahs of the world; between those who have more than what they need and those who have little or nothing; between those who direct their own lives and those who live at the fiat of others. The story of Hagar is clear: God has not forgotten Hagar.

God chooses Hagar as one of the four non-Jewish women of the Old Testament who, with Tamar, Rahab and Ruth, play a role in salvation history. It's so easy to think that the world is in the hands of those who think they control it. At every turn, however, are those who transcend the system and who, by their very distance from it, show it up for what it is. It is the poor of our societies who really show us the fibre of the society. It is the outcasts of a people who show us the real mettle of the people. It is the underclass of a society that is the measure of its upper class.

Finally, Hagar is the foreigner, the outcast woman, the lowest of the low, for whom God intervenes to give us a new insight into God. The fact is that God speaks to Hagar as clearly as God speaks to Abraham. The word of God, it seems, is not reserved for the patriarchs of any order. Women hear the word of God, and women carry it with them. Women are named by God as good, and, like Hagar, who called God 'one who sees me as I am,' women name God as well. Women name God liberator and life-giver and saviour in a world that oppresses them, uses up their lives without remorse, and leaves them to the mercy of the unjust and the unkind and the uncaring.

Hagar is the saint of hope and the icon of certainty. She gives us all a new way to look at the world around us, with its classes and laws and absolutes... She becomes the outcast companion of the living God and gives us all pause in the face of the poor. She raises the question of who is the judge of whom in a world where the manicured and sophisticated assume that God is on their side... Hagar is the saint for those who are tempted to think that God does not care.

Joan Chittister, *A Passion For Life: Fragments Of The Face Of God*, Orbis

HOW SHOULD WE VIEW THESE STORIES?

Although most scholars would now question the historicity of these passages from the Old Testament and see them as backward projections into a past about which the writers knew little (shown by various inaccuracies), nevertheless these are the mega-stories which, for Jew, Christian and indeed Muslim, bring inspiration. They are also stories which cause enormous conflict as to whether God promised the land to one group or another, when, for how long, and how much land. It's interesting to see that when Abraham and Lot's herdsmen fell out, the way to deal with the situation was a 'land for peace deal'! Maybe there will be lessons to learn which are both examples and also warnings, as we look at these ancient stories.

We shall see, as we journey on, that the situation is not solved by simply saying that the stories are historical, because this causes problems about the character of a God who calls for massacres. Hebron of the past and Hebron of the present reveal that this is still a problem.

Michael Prior, commenting on the promise of Abraham being the father of the multitudes and possessing the land says, 'Literary and historical investigation make it more likely that such promises emanated from within the ideologies of a much later period, perhaps that of the attempt to reconstitute national and religious identity in the wake of the Babylonian exile' (*The Bible and Colonialism*, Sheffield Academic Press, 1997). If indeed these are accounts written with a special intent, then they do help us when we come to the tribal conquests in Joshua 1—12 which seem to suggest that God is committed to genocide and leave us with a deep moral problem over the character of God. The archaeology of Palestine does not reflect the same picture as these writings, and seems to suggest that the origins of Israel were within Canaan, that there was no ethnic distinction between Canaanites and Israelites, and that there wasn't an invasion from outside. Consequently, the writers seem to have been trying to reflect more their contemporary needs for a sense of distinctiveness. They are therefore texts that belong 'to the genre of "myths of origin", which are encountered in virtually every society, and which... were deployed in the service of particular ideologies' (Michael Prior).

One could say that our understanding of God within the Bible is evolutionary and therefore that those who wrote these early passages had a limited understanding. Some of my Jewish friends seem to say this and they view the second part of Isaiah as the high moral and spiritual point of the Hebrew scriptures—a section, interestingly, to which Jesus repeatedly returns.

Most Liberation Theology naturally looks back to the Exodus model of liberation from Egypt but here, too, there is a problem. In Exodus 3:7–8 everyone stops after the words 'milk and honey'. 'I have observed the misery of my people who are in Egypt; I have heard their cry... I know their sufferings, and I have come down to deliver them from the Egyptians, and to bring them up out of that land to a land flowing with milk and honey.' But the verse goes on, '...to the country of the Canaanites, the Hittites, the Amorites, the Perizzites, the Hivites, and the Jebusites.' Because of this, some Jewish and Christian theologians now look to the post-exilic model for Liberation Theology rather than the Exodus model, because achieving one's own liberation at the expense of the oppression or domination of other groups naturally continues to provide an ongoing problem.

So in reading these passages we can be inspired and challenged, but also we need to be careful not to adopt attitudes that would reflect the character of an oppressive God rather than a liberating one.

HEBRON, LAND OF FRUIT AND MASSACRES

NUMBERS 13:17–18, 20, 22–23

Moses sent them to spy out the land of Canaan, and said to them, '...see what the land is like, and whether the people who live in it are strong or weak... Be bold, and bring some of the fruit of the land... They went up into the Negeb, and came to Hebron... (Hebron was built seven years before Zoan in Egypt.) And they came to the Wadi Eshcol, and cut down from there a branch with a single cluster of grapes, and they carried it on a pole between two of them. They also brought some pomegranates and figs.

JOSHUA 10:36–37, 40

Then Joshua went up with all Israel from Eglon to Hebron; they assaulted it, and took it, and struck it with the edge of the sword, and its king and its towns, and every person in it; he left no one remaining, just as he had done to Eglon, and utterly destroyed it with every person in it... So Joshua defeated the whole land... he left no one remaining, but utterly destroyed all that breathed.

If you look in the *Welcome to Palestine* brochure today under the section of Hebron, you will see that one of the local specialities is still fruit trees, along with olive groves and vineyards. Hebron is a fertile area. When Moses' spies came back with the fruit, they said that it was a land flowing with milk and honey and with fruit. They described it as a wonderful place but they were fearful of the communities living there. As a result they wandered in the wilderness with Moses and it was only Caleb and Joshua who were to lead them on the attack against Hebron. It is a chilling account in Joshua of the destruction of Hebron and the neighbouring towns. Verse after verse talks of the destruction of a new town and the death of everyone and every living thing within it. What is the character of a God who would order this? Again we have to look to those who wrote this book in later years and assume they were trying to teach something to their contemporaries about their community being distinctive. Nevertheless it is a disturbing story that would rarely be read in church. Its relevance is brought home in a contemporary story which shows the danger of having such a bloodthirsty concept of God.

On 25 February 1994, medical doctor Baruch Goldstein, a graduate of the most prestigious Yeshiva in the United States, massacred twenty-nine worshippers in the Ibrahimi mosque in Hebron. Naturally there was widespread revulsion, yet Dr Goldstein was steeped in the Bible, and at the time he did this it was the feast of Purim, when the book of Esther would be read—a book which celebrates the fight-back of the Jews. In the Siddur, the Jewish prayer book, there is a blessing that is recited on the feast of Purim, which talks of God exacting vengeance on Israel's foes, as indeed happened in the book of Esther. Obviously most people were appalled at this terrible massacre, yet there are others who revere Goldstein as a hero, particularly within the religious settler community, and especially in his own settlement at Kiryat Arba (which is the old name for Hebron). Goldstein's burial place, called Kahane Park, has become a shrine for pilgrims.

One of those who celebrated what Goldstein had done was Yigal Amir, the son of an Orthodox Rabbi, who was a student in advanced Torah studies at Bar-alan University. He was the man who killed the Prime Minister Yitzhak Rabin at the Tel Aviv Peace Rally on 4 November 1995, and claimed that he was acting 'in God's name'. In his room was found a book praising Goldstein. Just weeks before the assassination of the Prime Minister, a group of religious extremists had stood outside Rabin's house and cursed him: 'And on him, Yitzhak, son of Rosa, known as Rabin, we have permission… to demand from the angels the destruction that they take a sword to this wicked man… to kill him… for handing over the land of Israel to our enemies the sons of Ishmael' (Jewish Chronicle, 10 November 1995, p. 27). These people have been inspired by a view of God and religion that seems to give justification for massacre. Though most Jewish people would be appalled at this, it is the nature of the religious Jewish settlers who surround the indigenous Palestinian community in Hebron. The settlers are armed and extremist and, of course, the local community is not allowed to be armed. It is profoundly sad that this beautiful and fertile area should be a place of bloodshed and suffering. Here in Hebron, religion must be saved from its exclusivity.

Another Jewish person who has made a long-distance journey to Hebron is Rabbi Jeremy Milgrom, who has lived for many years in Israel, though he comes originally from the United States. Just after my latest visit (February 1998), Rabbi Jeremy and Rabbis for Human Rights joined the Christian Peacemakers in their stand at Hebron, and, where one home had been demolished, they started to rebuild for a Muslim family. This was even reported in the British press. Sadly, what wasn't reported was that, soon afterwards, the head of the household was arrested and beaten and the beginnings of his house were destroyed again. But there are seeds of hope in Hebron in people of the three faiths working together.

PRAYER
God-with-us, we give you praise and thanks for the blessings of this holy season. In Christ we have been given a new light that for ever shatters the power of evil. We acclaim Jesus as the hope of all the ages and the cause of our joy. The risen one goes before us and leads us to the day of your peace and reconciliation. Amen

Adapted from *Prayers For Dawn And Dusk* by Edward Gabriele, Saint Mary's Press, 1992

RABBIS FOR HUMAN RIGHTS

Rabbi Jeremy Milgrom is the co-ordinator of Rabbis for Human Rights. They have been demonstrating at Jabal abu Ghoneim (a beautiful hill overlooking Bethlehem) about the land being stripped to build the Har Homa settlement and have also been involved in trying to support those Palestinians and Bedouins whose homes have been demolished. Rabbi Jeremy says:

One thing I would say is that the public is not concerned enough and not active enough and although our group has had a renaissance in terms of activity, I think it's because of the cumulative efforts of some activists which have brought about a better coalition of networking, so that we can face issues like home demolitions. We're in a coalition that fights against home demolitions, but I would say that, by and large, people are not attentive enough, or even outraged enough, to effect change.

My hope for religion, and the way I would like to see it interact with the world in the future, is without the insecurities that religion has had. I think in terms of music: am I betraying my love of classical music if I listen to other music? Isn't it absurd? Would I ever buy a radio that could only pick up a classical music station? This is absurd. The way we think, the technology of our religious vocabulary, is so pitiful—in the way we tune out anything different than our own religious tradition. I think it's a terrible waste of our potential, of our spirituality, that we are so defensive about other traditions, we're so anxious, we're so worried. So my hope is that religions will learn how to contribute without feeling they have to fight for time, for turf or for legitimacy… they won't feel that they need to own anybody. They don't have to censor anyone else in order to be legit.

FRIDAY OF WEEK 1

JACOB AT BETHEL

GENESIS 35:1–3

God said to Jacob, 'Arise, go up to Bethel, and settle there. Make an altar there to the God who appeared to you when you fled from your brother Esau.' So Jacob said to his household and to all who were with him, 'Put away the foreign gods that are among you, and purify yourselves, and change your clothes; then come, let us go up to Bethel, that I may make an altar there to the God who answered me in the day of my distress and has been with me wherever I have gone.'

Jacob had been at Bethel before, and this chapter is a compilation of earlier incidents. In chapter 28, he called the place Bethel after having a dream of a ladder with angels ascending and descending. After that incident, he said the memorable words, 'How awesome is this place! This is none other than the house of God, and this is the gate of heaven' (28:17). He then set up a pillar, anointed it with oil and called the place Bethel. In chapter 35, Jacob comes to Bethel from Shechem (modern-day Nablus), where Jacob hid his household's foreign gods and earrings under an oak tree. Bethel is right next to modern-day Ramallah, which is one of the most thriving Palestinian towns on the West Bank. It's a town with a strong Christian heritage, but many Ramlawis (as the people of Ramallah are known) have emigrated to the United States.

In chapter 33, this tricky character—the name Jacob means 'supplanter'—has a dramatic encounter the other side of the Jordan, at the ford of Jabbok. Here Jacob seems to wrestle with an angel and refuses to let him go until the angel has blessed him. Because the angel can't prevail over Jacob, he touches Jacob's hip and puts it out of joint, and then says, 'Let me go, for the day is breaking.' But Jacob says, 'I will not let you go, unless you bless me.' He is then asked, 'What is your name?' and he replies, 'Jacob.' The angel says, 'You shall no longer be called Jacob, but Israel, for you have striven with God and with humans, and have prevailed.' There the angel blesses him. Jacob calls the place Peniel ('the face of God'), saying, 'For I have seen God face to face, and yet my life is preserved.' So Jacob limps away, after this remarkable imagery of a wrestle with God. It seems that it was a preparation for the next stage of his journey. The patriarchs have these extraordinary encounters: just as Abraham does with the three angels (or with God) at Mamre, so Jacob has this similar curious meeting in which he wrestles with an angel (or with God), and then is blessed.

There are people who tell you stories of encounters with God which are not unlike this, in which they have some way fought with God. I think of Father Miguel D'Escoto of Nicaragua. He is a remark-able man who served for twelve years as Foreign Minister in the Sandinista government. When Daniel Ortega—later to become President—called him to serve in Nicaragua, he was a religious book publisher in New York. He didn't want to go, partly because a revolutionary struggle was taking place—as a pacifist and a strong follower in the path of Jesus and of Martin Luther King, he felt he shouldn't be involved in it. But Daniel Ortega told him that this was fine, he would not be involved in the armed struggle. But what kind of society would they form when they came to power? Could he come and help them with that? He still resisted and didn't want to go, but he was made very conscious of the story of the Good Samaritan, where the priest passes by on the other side. As he described the story to me, it was almost as if he was having an argument with God, where God kept pointing out that his country and his people were lying wounded by the side of the road and that he was passing them by on the other side. What would that do for his people's understanding of the church and their understanding of God? So he went and he served in a government that had a particular commitment to the poor.

Although Father Miguel was out of government at the time I chatted with him, none of his zeal had abated and he talked about why there are few Christians in the West: '...because you keep Jesus Christ nailed up inside you, but you don't live his way.' Then he talked with admiration of Francis of Assisi and the way he had been 'a fool for Christ's sake', and he said that we need more people with those upside-down values. As I left him on that occasion, he went off to do a foolish thing for God. He and Daniel Ortega had bought a piece of land for the poor people. He pointed out that so often their land was poor in itself and unhealthy, maybe down by the river, and they'd bought a lovely piece of land and given it to various poor families. Unfortunately, the land was by the country club, and this meant that many wealthy people had driven them off it. As he walked away from us, he was going to intervene again on behalf of the poor. He was someone who had certainly been touched by God and who now lived out the gospel values.

PRAYER

You keep us waiting. You, the God of all time, want us to wait for the right time in which to discover who we are, where we must go, who will be with us, and what we must do. So thank you... for the waiting time.

You keep us looking. You, the God of all space, want us to look in the right and wrong places for signs of hope, for people who are hopeless, for visions of a better world which will appear among the disappointments of the world we know. So thank you... for the looking time.

You keep us loving. You, the God whose name is love, want us to be like you—to love the loveless and the unlovely and the unlovable; to love without jealousy or design or threat; and most difficult of all, to love ourselves. So thank you... for the loving time.

From the Iona Community Worship Book

Voices from Ramallah on Hope

First Voice: Cedar Duaybis

Cedar is a Palestinian Anglican and Secretary of the Board of Sabeel Ecumenical Liberation Centre.

All the main denominations are represented in Ramallah. The Orthodox is the biggest community and then the Latin church, which is smaller. There is also the Greek Catholic church, and then several Protestant churches of different denominations. There is an Anglican church, that is diminishing in number, to which I belong. People are leaving (i.e. to go abroad). At one time it used to be six hundred people, but now it is less than two hundred. But people still go to church and people are still attached to their churches.

Economically, the situation is worse than before the peace process started, and it's only a small fraction of the people who have money. The expected economic boom has not happened and there's recession, shops are empty and people are having difficulties.

However, we believe that God is a God of justice, and we believe that injustice cannot go on for ever. No matter how much it is suppressed, justice has a habit of rising again, so our hope is that our God is just. I personally have hope in the humanity of people and I always think that good will overcome evil, because there is no other solution for this country except for the two peoples to live together—the two peoples, the three faiths, to live together, otherwise there will be a disaster. So there's hope because sooner or later everybody's going to realize that this is the only way. This country is for all of us and we have to share it and live together in peace. I come from a generation that lived with Jews and Muslims before 1948 and I know how well it went and what a rich life we had, and what good Jewish and Muslim neighbours we had. So I always have this hope that this vision of the past is my dream for the future, and I think it's possible.

Second Voice: Naena Rabas

(A Christian Aid partner from Ramallah)

I am Naena Rabas from Ramallah, Palestine. I live around fifteen kilometres north of Jerusalem and I work with disabled people and do voluntary work with the ICC (International Christian Council) in Jerusalem, which serves the Palestinians in the West Bank. Most of our services are committed to children, mothers and youth. We're trying to create more new projects to help the needy people in Palestine to overcome their problems and to give them the support and therefore limit emigration of the Christians and the Palestinians from the land. Our major interest right now in planning for the five years to come is to help the youth to develop their skills to be the leaders of the future and to take care of most of the projects and services.

We're looking to the year 2000 with new spirit. We want to develop our faith, our interior faith, and look to other people as human beings and our brothers and sisters so that we can live together. We feel that we should be the supporters and the witness of Christianity in this area, and we hope that the next century would really be a peaceful century all over the world.

Third Voice: Dr Hanan Ashrawi

Dr Hanan was a peace negotiator in the Madrid Peace Talks and former cabinet member of the Palestinian National Authority. She is an Anglican Christian. Dr Hanan was asked what Christians might do to promote a just peace in the region.

I am glad that you have said 'just peace' because most people believe that peace is a process or a mechanism. They don't think of it as a state of being... that is based on a sense of justice. But we have to translate justice once again into workable habits. So I would say first of all that truth is on the side of a just peace. People have to always know the truth. They shouldn't be satisfied lightly. They shouldn't be satisfied with clichés, stereotypes or the racist generalizations that they were given... But once you have the truth you have a responsibility to act on it. I understand a contemporary church to be not only a contemplative church but also an active church with a sense of social responsibility, for social justice internally and for humanity. I am saying that we do share a collective responsibility. If we want to translate a genuine peace into reality, we should be intolerant of injustice. I believe that the courage to stand up and speak out, even when it is not very popular or very rewarding in terms of daily events and realities... ultimately involves a process of redemption. I believe that it can be done, the churches should be able to speak out, should reach out.

Cornerstone Easter 1997, published by Sabeel Liberation Theology Centre

RACHEL'S TOMB

GENESIS 35:16–20, 27, 29

Then they journeyed from Bethel; and when they were still some distance from Ephrath, Rachel was in childbirth, and she had hard labour. When she was in her hard labour, the midwife said to her, 'Do not be afraid; for now you will have another son.' As her soul was departing (for she died), she named him Ben-oni (son of my sorrow); but his father called him Benjamin (son of the right hand). So Rachel died, and she was buried on the way to Ephrath (that is, Bethlehem), and Jacob set up a pillar at her grave; it is the pillar of Rachel's tomb, which is there to this day... Jacob came to his father Isaac at Mamre, or Kiriath-arba (that is, Hebron), where Abraham and Isaac had resided as aliens... And Isaac breathed his last; he died and was gathered to his people, old and full of days; and his sons Esau and Jacob buried him.

As you come into Bethlehem on the Jerusalem road, you pass the traditional burial place for Rachel. Revered by Jews, there has been a succession of synagogues on the site, although it's also holy to Muslims, as a cemetery of the Bedouin Ta'amre tribe lies in the grounds. Between 1948 and 1967 the site was protected by the Islamic Waqf and was open to Jewish worshippers. Today it is under permanent guard by Israeli soldiers. Rabbi Jeremy Milgrom says of it:

Today Rachel's Tomb has been turned into a fortress—it's a monument to our insecurity, to our inability to recognize the Palestinians would respect Jewish yearnings and worship and attachment to a holy site. If only we allow them to do that and not turn it into another act of 'this is mine' and 'I'm gonna call the shots'. My Palestinian friend Omar mentioned to me the other day that they used to call the tomb 'our mother'—that this was shorthand for the tomb. Now we could all relate to Rachel as our mother, and then we would be one step closer to understanding.

It is strange that a place where many women go to pray is such a symbol of religious aggression and becomes a regular place of conflict. Women seem to come here to pray either that they might have a child or perhaps, because the reference on the wall is from Jeremiah 31:15–17, it may also be to pray for the protection of children, particularly those serving in the army.

When we visited Rachel's Tomb, as we walked away we picked up bullet shells from the other side of the road and gas canisters that had been fired by the Israeli army. Religion can possess people in a way that causes them to oppress others. On my latest visit to the Holy Land, I met several people of different religious backgrounds who had given up on faith because they saw it brought such pain and suffering with it. There are those of us who would like to say, 'Hold on to your spirituality', but how can we say that unless it's a faith that liberates rather than oppresses?

In this first week of Advent, we have come across a couple of religious sites which have been places of conflict, namely the burial place of the patriarchs and Rachel's Tomb. On our journey, as we look at signposts pointing to Bethlehem, and to the birth there, we will see the clues to a spirituality that rejects domination and oppression, violence and the gun. Spirituality encapsulated in the child of Bethlehem will go any distance, take any path of suffering, even the way of the cross, to avoid the route of domination and to hear the cry of, and stand with, those who are forgotten and suffering.

LIGHTING THE CANDLE

Light a candle for this week and for the people you've met on your journey this week. Light a candle for those who live in the shadow of the settlers in Hebron. Remember the Christian Peacemaker Team and pray for them in their witness to this Muslim town. Pray for Rabbi Jeremy Milgrom and the Rabbis for Human Rights as they show such a different Jewish spirituality from the extremism of the settlers.

Look back to Sunday. Did you write down a name of somebody for whom you would be lighting a candle?

ADVENT 2

Come, Lord Jesus

ADVENT ECUMENICAL BIBLE STUDIES

I belong to the movement of the Palestinian Ecumenical Liberation Theology group, the Sabeel Centre. During Advent we have special Bible studies. Our Bible studies are different from just ordinary Bible studies because we struggle with passages from the Hebrew scriptures and try to interpret them with Palestinian reality, but still from the viewpoint of faith. I think they are very, very interesting. So in Advent, and in Lent, we hold Bible studies that people from all denominations come to, and I really look forward to them. Every time we have them something new emerges. Ordinary people are capable of thinking and reflecting theologically... on the times we live, and finding good news and hope in our holy book.

Cedar Duaybis

ADVENT—A TIME FOR SURRENDER

Advent is the time for rousing. We are shaken to the very depths, so that we may wake up to the truth of ourselves. The primary condition for a fruitful and rewarding Advent is renunciation, surrender. We must let go of all our mistaken dreams, our conceited poses and arrogant gestures, all the pretences with which we hope to deceive ourselves and others. If we fail to do this, stark reality may take hold of us and rouse us forcibly in a way that will entail both anxiety and suffering.

Alfed Delp, from *The Prison Meditations of Father Delp*, Herder and Herder, 1968

JEROME AND THE BIBLE

MARK 12:24, 27–31

Jesus said to them, '... you know neither the scriptures nor the power of God' ... 'He is God not of the dead, but of the living.' ... One of the scribes... asked him, 'Which commandment is the first of all?' Jesus answered, 'The first is, "Hear, O Israel: the Lord our God, the Lord is one; you shall love the Lord your God with all your heart, and with all your soul, and with all your mind, and will all your strength." The second is this, "You shall love your neighbour as yourself." There is no other commandment greater than these.'

This Sunday of Advent is kept as Bible Sunday in many churches, and so it is a good time to think about Jerome, who translated the Bible in Bethlehem. In AD382, Pope Damasus commissioned Jerome to produce a Latin Bible, and from 386 to 404 Jerome translated the Bible from Hebrew and Greek into Latin. The outcome of this was the Vulgate which, for the next 1,500 years, would be the official Bible of the Roman Catholic Church. Jerome also wrote numerous commentaries on particular books such as the prophets and the epistles, and his commentary on Matthew's Gospel became a standard work.

Jerome was helped by Paula and Eustochium who, with him, founded the Christian monastic communities around Bethlehem. Paula was a great fan of Bethlehem and said, 'Yes, this will be my resting place; since the Redeemer himself has chosen this as his residence, this is where I too want to stay.' Her grave, and that of her daughter, can be found in the same crypt, close to the Grotto of the Nativity. The cave of Jerome, where he translated the Bible, is beneath the Church of the Nativity and directly connected to the cave where Jesus is thought to have been born. Upstairs now in the Church of the Nativity, there is a beautiful cloister dedicated to Jerome, and there is a statue of him in the garden there, dating from about 1880.

Our passage today reflects Jesus' use of the Jewish scriptures in discussion with Sadducees and scribes. First of all, the Sadducees have been trying to catch Jesus out with a rather ridiculous suggested scenario in which a woman is married to seven brothers in succession. Jesus points out that when they rise from the dead, there will be a new situation. Although the Sadducees would have been known as highly literate men, he accuses them of ignorance of both the scriptures and the power of God. He then addresses their doubt about the resurrection from the dead and points out that God is the God of the living.

Jesus is then tested by the scribes. He knows the right answer to their question and quotes the *Shema* (the Jewish prayer from Deuteronomy 6:6–9), though he boldly links it with the words from the Levitical code of justice about loving our neighbour—which implies that to love God is to refuse to exploit one's neighbour. Jesus quotes from Leviticus 19:18, and the verses around this passage make a commentary on that verse. The Israelites are called to be generous and just with their neighbours, with the poor and with the alien. They are not to steal or defraud one another or to swear falsely. They are not to defraud their neighbour, they are not to keep the wages of a labourer until the following morning, they are not to mistreat the deaf or the blind, or to render unjust judgments, or to slander, or to take vengeance or to bear a grudge. The scribe responds that Jesus is right and even echoes a passage from Micah (6:6–8) that loving one's neighbour is more important than burnt offerings and sacrifices. Jesus recognizes this and tells him, 'You are not far from the kingdom of God.'

Jesus then goes on to talk about the scribes and asks how they can say that 'the Messiah is the son of David'. The scribes assumed that the Messiah would restore the Davidic monarchy and that they in turn would find their own position strengthened, but Jesus points out that even David is subordinate to God's sovereignty. As his ride into Jerusalem on a donkey later revealed, Jesus had no interest in building up dreams of a Davidic empire because he saw the politics of domination to be the problem. His rebuttal of the scribes brings delight to the crowd. Jesus is not afraid to use the scriptures to correct wrong views, even if the scriptures are quoted at him. Jesus will not let scripture become an instrument that oppresses, but rather a source that shows people how to live, how to have their hopes raised, how to treat their neighbour, and how to walk on the path of liberation.

BETHLEHEM BIBLE COLLEGE

Following in the footsteps of Jerome, there is a Bible College in Bethlehem, which has been there for eighteen years and is encouraging people's understanding of the Bible. Bishara Awad is the Principal and he says:

I see Bethlehem as a place of good news, a place where the Word became flesh and God himself came and dwelt among us. We are approaching the year 2000 and we want to re-enact the message of good news from Bethlehem to the whole world and to tell the people that Jesus is alive and there is hope, there is salvation, and it all started from here in Bethlehem.

We, as Palestinians, are not sure what our future will be, but as Christians I say we have our hope in the Lord. He is the Lord of history. We know things will turn around and we pray that there will be a change of heart. The whole town of Bethlehem is under siege, no one is allowed to leave except with the written permission of the military governor, so the situation is quite sad. But that cannot continue and we are a people of hope. We look for a brighter day that will come. We pray that that day will come soon.

PRAYER

Blessed Lord, who caused all holy scriptures to be written for our learning: help us so to hear them, to read, mark, learn and inwardly digest them that, through patience and the comfort of your holy word, we may embrace and for ever hold fast the hope of everlasting life, which you have given us in our Saviour Jesus Christ.

Collect for Bible Sunday, 2nd Sunday of Advent (*Alternative Service Book 1980*)

MONDAY OF WEEK 2

MARY'S SONG AT EIN KAREM

LUKE 1:39–41, 46–55

In those days Mary set out and went with haste to a Judean town in the hill country, where she entered the house of Zechariah and greeted Elizabeth. When Elizabeth heard Mary's greeting, the child leaped in

her womb... And Mary said, 'My soul magnifies the Lord, and my spirit rejoices in God my Saviour, for he has looked with favour on the lowliness of his servant. Surely, from now on all generations will call me blessed; for the Mighty One has done great things for me, and holy is his name. His mercy is for those who fear him from generation to generation. He has shown strength with his arm; he has scattered the proud in the thoughts of their hearts. He has brought down the powerful from their thrones, and lifted up the lowly; he has filled the hungry with good things, and sent the rich away empty. He has helped his servant Israel, in remembrance of his mercy, according to the promise he made to our ancestors, to Abraham and to his descendants forever.'

The setting for the Magnificat is traditionally the village of Ein Karem, about seven kilometres west of Jerusalem. Here, it's believed, was the traditional home of Zechariah and Elizabeth. Here Mary came to visit Elizabeth when she was expecting John, and when Mary had discovered that she also was pregnant. It's in this context that the extraordinary and radical words of the Magnificat are spoken. One of the Holy Land guides says, 'Looking at the Church of the Visitation is probably one of the most beautiful of all the gospel sites in the Holy Land. This peaceful setting is an excellent place for meditation.' This reflects accurately one of the deep problems of touring round the Holy Land. The village of Ein Karem has a far from peaceful history and to meditate here on words from the Bible, in isolation from the reality of what has happened in this place, is, in fact, to lose sight of the extraordinary significance of the Magnificat and its deep commitment to justice. My Christian Aid colleague, Tony Graham, has written some deeply moving words about visiting Ein Karem in his book, *With Sure Fierce Love Towards Galilee* (published 1998):

In January 1995 we visited Ein Karem, walking up to the church in the hilly country of Judea where Mary hastened to greet Elizabeth. There were almond trees about to blossom on the old terraces below. Around the courtyard Mary's song was displayed on tablets in every language and the singing of Magnificat in church was lovely. Walking down to the bus, Hanna our guide told us that the fine Arab houses had been left empty after the fighting of 1948, so the place had been occupied by a colony of artists. It was all a delightful religious experience.

But exactly a year later I had another story in my mind. At the conference run by Sabeel, the centre that exists to give hope to Palestinian Christians, we had heard how on 9 April 1948 Menachem Begin's men, following plan Dalet, attacked the nearby village of Deir Yassin in the night and killed 254 children, women and men. The men were killed after they'd been paraded round the city. The bodies were thrown down the village well. The next day, 10 April, the soldiers came to Ein Karem and warned the people of a like fate if they did not leave their homes immediately. The parish priest of this largely Christian village led his people over the hill towards Bethlehem and into exile. And that is why two magnificent churches in Ein Karem have no congregation today beyond the stream of pilgrims... I met a charming French Franciscan and asked him if there was any remembering of these events at the shrine today; any attempt to pray healing prayers. No there is not... I went to the crypt chapel of John the Baptist. There—on the wall—was painted the dreadful killing of children—a backdrop to the miraculous preservation of Jesus showing the massacre of the innocents, and I found myself praying the only prayer I could and wept for all the pain covered up by layers of religion. For all the innocents—those of Deir Yassin, and of all such places... As I came out, a group were reciting Mary's song. 'He has put down the mighty from their thrones, and exalted those of low degree; he has filled the hungry with good things...' At Ein Karem religion is strong and the hope of the dispossessed seems hopeless, cocooned in piety. And yet across the valley from the church we can see Deir Yassin, a perpetual reproach to comfortable religion. Just over the shoulder of the hill—up to the top on the bus and just a short walk down—is a place called Yad Vashem.

I took the first available opportunity to see Yad Vashem (the Jewish Holocaust Memorial). The memorial to the children is a shattering experience, Struggling through darkness, one and a half million children. An infinity of candle flames. The measured reciting of the names and the place each of them called home; a journey through the heart of darkness till suddenly we are out in the light again. Here there ought to be a place to sit, kneel, pray, scream; such things must never happen again!

But a sign invites us to move on to the valley of the destroyed communities. Behind a screen of trees the valley drops down. And there across the valley is Deir Yassin... where the expulsion and killing of people for being the wrong race did not stop but continued. It continued through Ein Karem, along the valley path to Bethlehem and onward, those that survived, to the camps. Through Beit Sahour where the angels sang of peace, and through Bethlehem they went. To the camps that still remain in Gaza and Jericho, to the Lebanon and Syria and onward to exile.

Tony Graham, *With Sure Fierce Love Towards Galilee*, 1998

So, Ein Karem, a place that starts with such vision, with Mary's song, becomes a place that points us to Deir Yassin, which in turn points us to Yad Vashem, which in turn points us to Auschwitz Birkenau. It was standing in Auschwitz Birkenau that I felt the challenge that we must never again let these events of horror happen. We must never again be quiet about injustice, genocide, ethnic cleansing. It's here at Ein Karem that we can be restored with the vision of the kind of society and community we should be, and the nature of the God we follow, who scatters the proud, brings down the powerful, lifts up the lowly, fills the hungry and sends the rich away empty.

What a compassionate God. In this remarkable song we can only say, 'Come, Lord Jesus,' come to our places of pain and bring healing, come to our wounded memories and bring healing. Come to this world that has shed so much blood—too much blood—and bring healing and the commitment that we must never let these things happen again.

PRAYER
Pray today for the displaced Palestinian refugees, for the two wounded communities of Palestinians and Jews, and also take some time to pray about issues that are in the news at the moment where there are places of conflict, war or suffering. And pray the values of Mary's song into these situations with the words, 'Come, Lord Jesus.'

HASSAN'S RAINBOW HOPE

Hassan Newash, a Palestinian engineer now living in the United States, was born in Ein Karem. He's a refugee, and he lives in Michigan and works with a group of Palestinians and Jews, particularly on the issue of Jerusalem—that it should be kept as an open city. He is trying to guard against the erosion of Jerusalem into an exclusively Jewish city. He's a Muslim, and I asked him, 'Can people of faith have hope?' He said:

For me, I think the backbone of our relationship should be the worthiness of the human being, irrespective of his or her religious beliefs. I'm still worthy whether I am Christian, Muslim or Jew, or an atheist for that matter—there is sacredness to the life of a human being and we should honour that soul as such, no matter what the beliefs. I don't see that respect in allowing only Jews to come in under the law of return, while depriving Palestinian refugees from coming back. I believe this should be changed.

I profess that kind of hope and vision that believes there is an openness in Islam to be in a relationship of one human being to another, and an equal basis where all draw resources from the land, and we celebrate our plurality of differences rather than concentrating on the ethnocentric kind of emphasis. For me, diversity is beautiful and we should nurture relationships based on that and that's my vision.

TUESDAY OF WEEK 2

BETHLEHEM—
BY NO MEANS LEAST

MICAH 5:2, 4–5
But you, O Bethlehem of Ephrathah, who are one of the little clans of Judah, from you shall come forth for me one who is to rule in Israel, whose origin is from of old, from ancient days… And he shall stand and feed his flock in the strength of the Lord… and he shall be the one of peace.

The Gospel of Matthew sees these words as significant. When the wise men come looking for Jesus, and Herod enquires where the Messiah is to be born, it is this passage which they quote. To Matthew this is particularly important because Bethlehem is David's city and this is where the successor to David will come from. The successor to David will stand and feed his flock in Bethlehem just as David the shepherd boy had done, and yet, as we see at the end of this passage, he shall be the one of peace. David was a man of war, who was not allowed to build the temple because he had been such a warrior, but this one would bring wholeness to the community.

In Bethlehem today there are those who follow in this same pathway of peace. One of these is Zoughbi Zoughbi, the Director of the Palestinian Centre for Conflict Resolution (Wi'am). Zoughbi talked about the work of Wi'am:

Wi'am means 'cordial relationships' and you can tell our emphasis from the term we use. Our whole work focuses on relationships and, despite the lack of progress in the peace process, despite the negative atmosphere and the unemployment, we thought it was good to start doing a positive approach and to be with people and to invest in the quality of relationship among people. So in this place what we do is try to respond to people's needs, to be there when they ask us to be, and to respond in resolving conflicts. For us, conflict resolution is the art and work of sharing yourself, your resources, your mind, your heart and your emotions with the people. Our one work here is mediation. We try to help shape our society into a more pluralistic democratic society.

Zoughbi knows the desperate mood of Bethlehem at the moment and the difficulties under which people live. Many might still consider it to be a place of no significance, but Bethlehem still has an extra-ordinary role to play. At the time of the millennium, eyes are fixed on Bethlehem and it is important to say to the people of Bethlehem, 'You are still by no means the least.' Though it looks as if you are forgotten by the world, though you're squeezed and oppressed, you still have something to teach us all, particularly in the style and the message of the one who came humbly to a cave in Bethlehem and thereby turned all our values upside-down. As Canon Naim Ateek has said, powerful leaders who visit Jerusalem often 'come with the illusion that the answers to peace lie with the Herods in Jerusalem'. But he says that it would be better for 'today's magi to visit Bethlehem. They do not realize that the genuine answers to peace lie in everything the child of Bethlehem has stood for: humility, openness, love of others, forgiveness, even sacrifice of oneself for others.'

PRAYER

*Thank you for Bethlehem. Thank you for the Christian community of
Bethlehem. Thank you for the message of Bethlehem, the house of bread,
and for the way it feeds us all. And into present day suffering, come, Lord
Jesus. Come with your simplicity, your upside-down values, to restore
hope, where angels once sang of peace. Come to those sitting by their
demolished houses on the hills surrounding Bethlehem and Hebron.
Come, Lord Jesus, to our broken world. Come, Lord Jesus, with the bread
of life. Amen*

BETHLEHEM NOW

Zoughbi Zoughbi explained to me some of the day-to-day difficulties
of living in Bethlehem at the moment. There is a deteriorating
economy; the standard of living has dropped drastically;
unemployment is skyrocketing; there is a lack of freedom of
movement because of 'closure', and a lack of water, and so there is a
feeling of depression, frustration, and waiting for something to
happen. He is particularly concerned because he feels the margin of
hope is getting smaller and people are becoming angry. He says, 'The
closure is really a kind of pressure cooker in which we are now living.'

I thought it would be helpful to get Zoughbi to define three key
contemporary issues for Bethlehem.

Closure

Zoughbi pointed out that there is a double type of closure imposed
upon them, the first an external closure, and the second an internal
one called 'siege'. The external closure is to prevent the local
community from moving freely to Jerusalem, the Gaza Strip or from
south to north via Jerusalem. The siege is to prevent people from
moving from one town to another within the West Bank. When there
is a closure, people can't go to work and have no access to any kind
of activity, including going to school or to hospital.

Areas A, B and C

Zoughbi explained that with the peace process has come the division
of the land into areas A, B and C. Area A is controlled by the
Palestinian authority. Area B is jointly controlled by Palestinian and

Israeli, with security being handled by Israel and the civil services by the Palestinians. Area C is under Israeli control. 'So, with the peace process, we only have control of three per cent of the West Bank, which is Area A.' (This could change if the Wye Agreement is implemented: the maximum they could have under Wye would be 18.5 per cent.)

Jabal Abu Ghoneim
(visible on the front cover of this book)

A name that keeps cropping up if you visit Bethlehem is the hill of Jabal Abu Ghoneim, or Har Homa. This is the hill where a housing settlement of some 8,500 is proposed by the Israelis. There are also plans for a tourist centre, with hotels, shopping malls and recreational areas. This would take away whatever is left of the tourist economy from the existing Bethlehem area, which has already been eroded by the confiscation of land. Zoughbi says, 'Sixty per cent of the Bethlehem area has been confiscated since 1967 and 96 per cent of the land belonged to the Christians; this explains why so many Christians are leaving.'

WEDNESDAY OF WEEK 2

DON'T LOOK ON THE OUTWARD APPEARANCE

1 SAMUEL 16: 1, 6–7, 10–12

The Lord said to Samuel, 'How long will you grieve over Saul? I have rejected him from being king over Israel. Fill your horn with oil and set out; I will send you to Jesse the Bethlehemite, for I have provided for myself a king among his sons.' ... When they came, he looked on Eliab and thought, 'Surely the Lord's anointed is now before the Lord.' But the Lord said to Samuel, 'Do not look on his appearance or on the height of his stature, because I have rejected him; for the Lord does not see as mortals see; they look on the outward appearance, but the Lord looks on the heart.' ... Jesse made seven of his sons pass before Samuel, and Samuel said to Jesse, 'The Lord has not chosen any of these.' Samuel said to Jesse, 'Are all your sons here?' And he said, 'There remains yet the youngest, but he is keeping the sheep.' And Samuel said to Jesse, 'Send and bring him; for we will not sit down until he comes here.' He sent and brought him in. Now he was ruddy, and had beautiful eyes, and was handsome. The Lord said, 'Rise and anoint him; for this is the one.'

This is a remarkable passage. God, who had originally tried to suggest to the people of Israel that they should not have a king, had eventually given in and allowed Saul to be their king. (God is clearly a republican, but will relent on occasions!) But now we see reflected something of God's character—that the Lord doesn't see as humans do. God doesn't look just on the outward appearance but looks on the heart. To the amazement of Jesse, none of his other sons, who had appeared eminently suitable, are chosen, but the one they would otherwise have forgotten—a musician, a poet, and a shepherd. It's really with Samuel's visit to Bethlehem, the sacrifice he made and the anointing of David here, that Bethlehem comes to occupy a unique place in religious life.

David's name is unique in the scripture and reminds us of the special place he has as ancestor of Jesus. There are fifty-eight New Testament references to David, including the title given to Jesus, which was often repeated, 'Son of David'. Just as David came from Bethlehem, so Jesus was born there both to fulfil the words of the prophet Micah and to show that he was in the line of David and a king like David.

My son, Tom, works with street kids in South Africa. When he was working in East London, South Africa, at a project called Isaiah 58, a young girl came to the project who had been abused and treated very badly. Tom found it very hard to get her to respond at first. He was studying Xhosa at the time and discovered that her name, Nombitshi, meant 'ugly'. It was a nickname she had been given and showed just how little she had been valued before. He also discovered that by a subtle change in Xhosa, her name could be made to say 'beautiful'—by changing it to Nomhle. So on one occasion, almost as if it was an accident, he called her Nomhle. He told me, 'She couldn't wipe the grin off her face.' A few days later Tom and the other staff were called down to the school and told that Nombitshi wanted to change her name. He still wasn't sure what name she wanted because Nombitshi was her nickname and he wondered if she wanted to go back to her original name. But they called her in and asked her and she said, no, she wanted to be called Nomhle.

It's so easy to dismiss people, to look on the outward appearances, to write somebody off and not see their potential, to say someone is 'ugly' or 'nobody'—whereas God says they are 'beautiful' and 'somebody'. God saw Nomhle's potential. Her nickname may have been 'ugly', but God saw that she was 'beautiful'.

PRAYER
Lord, teach us to see the potential in every human being, to see people as you do, to treasure them as people made in your image. Amen

TO DO
Today, using the 'Come, Lord Jesus' prayer, it would be good to think of individuals you know in whom it's particularly hard to recognize their potential or the good in them. Pray for the coming of the Lord Jesus into their situation and for people to recognize their potential, their value, and their worth, and to see them with the eyes of God.

AT HOME IN BETHLEHEM

I have been in the homes of both the rich and poor in Bethlehem. I have been in the mansions of the merchants and olive-wood carvers, and I have sat in the homes of people who barely have a door to close against the cold, damp winters of the Judean hills. Yet here in this tiny town, one can still find the Christian faith alive and well, living and breathing in the lives of Arab Christians who make Bethlehem their home. Despite the difficulties of life in this city, I have found people as dedicated to their faith as anyone could hope to find. Regardless of the tragedies, difficulties and obstacles that have beset them, the people of Bethlehem have somehow maintained a glimmer of hope in the midst of hopelessness; joy in the face of despair; and dignity in a part of the world that has denied them recognition for so long.

When I was a child, Bethlehem was a place that existed only in beautifully illustrated pictures of Bible story books—a place that existed far away and was only reflected upon every year as 25 December approached. But here in Bethlehem, the miracle of that first Christmas is remembered every day of the year... Bethlehem, spiritual home to Christians the world over, has, for the last year, been my physical home. Here, in a place that could offer no room for the Christ-child, I have found both room and acceptance from a people who live daily the message brought to earth nearly two thousand years ago.

Douglas Dicks, a Presbyterian missionary seconded to the Middle East Council of Churches Jerusalem office, from the MECC NewsReport Jan–Feb 1997

A SHORT HISTORY OF BETHLEHEM

Bethlehem is thought to have been inhabited since the Stone Age and certainly we know that it was already a settlement three thousand years before the birth of Christ. Canaanite tribes had built small cities surrounded by walls for protection against the attacks of outsiders. One of these cities was Beit Lahama, which we know as Bethlehem. There was a temple for the Chaldean god of fertility, called Lahama, built on the present mount of the Nativity. It had a good view over the fertile valleys of the region, which is the area we now know as the Shepherds' Fields.

Bethlehem was mentioned around 1350BC in the Tell al-Amarna letters from the Egyptian governor of Palestine to Amenhotep III. It was depicted then as an important rest stop for travellers from Syria and Palestine going to Egypt.

The Philistines had come into the land of the Canaanites and had achieved military supremacy over the greater part of the country by around 1200BC. They called the land Palestine. The struggle between the Philistines and the Israelites is reflected in the Bible, and from the first book of the Bible Bethlehem is mentioned. The New Testament stories are well known but after that, in AD135, the Emperor Hadrian turned the Grotto of the Nativity in Bethlehem into a pagan sanctuary and had a grove of trees planted over the Grotto. Justin Martyr, in AD155, refers to the Bethlehem cave where Jesus was born and talks about it being surrounded by a grove dedicated to Adonis. The writer Oregin in 215 talks in the same way. From 315 onwards, some sort of church or basilica has been here. In 325, the Bishop of Jerusalem, Marcarius, informed Emperor Constantine about the neglected condition of the holy places. Constantine ordered that churches should be built in certain places, and they included the Church of the Nativity.

The Church of the Nativity is the oldest complete church in the world. There is a story that when the Persians destroyed all the Christian buildings in the Holy Land at the beginning of the seventh century, they recognized on the west wall of the church a representation of the three wise men in costumes of their own country. Consequently, in respect for their own ancestors, they spared the basilica from destruction. For security reasons, the entrance to the church has become smaller and smaller, and as you stand up when you come inside you see an interior which hasn't changed very much since the Emperor Justinian constructed it in the sixth century. There is no furniture in the nave, and there is a beautiful atmosphere in this church.

Historically, the Church of the Nativity has been a place of peace between Christians and Muslims. In 637 the Muslim Khalif Umar Ibn al-Khattab came to Bethlehem and prayed in the basilica. Consequently, a written agreement was reached with the patriarch Sofronious that Muslims would pray in the church as individuals and they would use the southern apse which was orientated towards Mecca, while Christians cared for the building's maintenance. From then on, Bethlehem was in various hands, including the crusaders, Saladin, the Mamluks and the Turks, and even the Egyptians at one point. After the Balfour Declaration in 1917, the Jews were given the right to form a national home in Palestine as long as the rights of the original people of the country were respected. In 1918 Palestine was placed under the British Mandate and in 1948 Bethlehem came under the union of the Eastern part of Palestine and Trans-Jordan. In 1967 the Israelis occupied the remainder of Palestine, including Bethlehem, and on 22 December 1995 the Palestinian Authority took over Bethlehem in line with the Oslo Accord.

I am grateful to Sawsan and Qustandi Shomali's Official Guide *Bethlehem 2000—A Guide To Bethlehem And Its Surroundings*, which is a particularly helpful little book, for much of the information in this short history.

RUTH COMES TO BETHLEHEM

RUTH 1:19–22

So the two of them went on until they came to Bethlehem. When they came to Bethlehem, the whole town was stirred because of them; and the women said, 'Is this Naomi?' She said to them, 'Call me no longer Naomi, call me Mara, for the Almighty has dealt bitterly with me. I went away full, but the Lord has brought me back empty; why call me Naomi when the Lord has dealt harshly with me, and the Almighty has brought calamity upon me?' So Naomi returned together with Ruth the Moabite, her daughter-in-law, who came back with her from the country of Moab. They came to Bethlehem at the beginning of the barley harvest.

One of the intentions of this beautiful and very moving little story is to say to the Jewish community, in the post-exilic period in which it was written, that non-Jews were acceptable to Yahweh. It was a time when intermarriage was both convenient and probably common, but many deemed it to be wrong. The book of Ruth stands as a reminder that non-Jewish people were not to be condemned. We shall see later how in the genealogy of Jesus several non-Jewish people are included. David was very accepting of the Jebusites when he took Jerusalem. He was generous to the Jebusite king, who was allowed to keep his estate outside the city wall, and he also maintained the Jebusite administration. David also seems to have married a Jebusite woman so even Solomon was half Jebusite. Most significant of all, it looks as if Zadok the chief priest was a Jebusite, as this is a Jebusite name. Perhaps it's not surprising that the book of Ruth ends with a reminder that Ruth is an ancestor of David (4:17–20).

Ruth the Moabite had married the son of Naomi. When Naomi's husband and two sons had died and she was deciding to go back to her own family in Bethlehem, Ruth insisted on going with her, and said those beautiful words, 'Do not press me to leave you or to turn back from following you! Where you go, I will go; where you lodge, I will lodge; your people shall be my people, and your God my God. Where you die, I will die—there will I be buried' (Ruth 1:16–17). Ruth's affection for Naomi brings her then to Bethlehem at the beginning of the barley harvest and this little detail sets the scene for the romance that is to follow. Naomi is in some ways a broken woman. She says, 'I went away full, but the Lord has brought me back empty.' The first chapter of Ruth has a particular emphasis on loss: for Naomi there is loss of food which forces her, with her husband, to leave her homeland and live in Moab, where loss of husband and loss of sons occurs. Ruth, in turn, loses her husband and her homeland. Moab provides a family from Bethlehem with food during a famine but it's to Bethlehem ('house of bread')—Naomi's home town—that she longs to return to rebuild her life.

There are deep echoes of the contemporary situation in Naomi's words. So many people living in this area were driven out from other towns or have lost close friends and relatives and now try to rebuild their community in a town that is shrinking before their eyes. There are different strands in the Old Testament that reflect the character of God in different ways and were probably written at different times, but here we are a long way from the God who talks to Joshua and tells him to kill every living thing, Instead we now find the character of God that is accepting of all. From the Christian point of view, to look back at Ruth is fascinating because she is in the genealogy not only of David but also of Jesus. The Gospel writer Matthew is very keen to point this out and, of course, Bethlehem figures large in all their lives.

PRAYER
Today, particularly focus your thoughts on someone who, like Naomi, may find their life suddenly to be empty, and pray 'Come, Lord Jesus' into this person, into this situation. Also think of refugees, homeless people, displaced people, those suffering from famine or bereavement. Think of those who have lived for years in the refugee camps in Bethlehem, and pray that the values prophesied and promised at the birth of Jesus—peace and justice—will come to Bethlehem.

Harvest Time at the House of Bread

Ruth 2:1–6, 8, 10–12 (abridged)

Now Naomi had a kinsman on her husband's side, whose name was Boaz. And Ruth the Moabite said to Naomi, 'Let me go to the field and glean among the ears of grain, behind someone in whose sight I may find favour.' She said to her, 'Go, my daughter.' So she went. She came and gleaned in the field behind the reapers. As it happened, she came to the part of the field belonging to Boaz. Just then Boaz came from Bethlehem… Boaz said to his servant, 'To whom does this young woman belong?' The servant answered, 'She is the Moabite who came back with Naomi from the country of Moab.' … Then Boaz said to Ruth, 'Now listen, my daughter, do not go to glean in another field.' Then she said to him, 'Why have I found favour in your sight, when I am a foreigner?' Boaz answered her, 'All that you have done for your mother-in-law has been fully told me. May you have a full reward from the Lord, the God of Israel, under whose wings you have come for refuge!'

So the 'house of bread' is now to supply the necessary food. Into this harvest situation comes Boaz. He spots Ruth immediately, he enters the field and discovers that she is the Moabite whom he had heard so much about from Naomi. He is concerned that she should be treated properly. Later he asks her to come and eat with him. She eats till she is satisfied and then Boaz also instructs his workers that she is to glean among the standing sheaves and that they are to pull some handfuls out for her so that there is plenty for her to pick up. Naomi spots that she has a tremendous amount of barley and asks, 'Where did you glean?' She says, 'Boaz's field' and Naomi is delighted because he is such a near relative.

Naomi then sets about a matchmaking role and sends a smartly dressed and perfumed Ruth to lie at Boaz's feet. He is surprised and impressed, particularly because, as he says, 'You have not gone after young men.' But he recognizes that he is not her nearest kinsman and so he must ask another one who is more closely related. Boaz then gives her more barley because he says she must not go back to Naomi empty-handed.

There is a hint here that Naomi, who came to Bethlehem empty, is not to remain so. Food has been restored, lack of which was the very reason she left to go to Moab, and now perhaps a potential spouse is in sight for Ruth, which would bring the hope of descendants. If this were to happen, Naomi's emptiness would be made full.

THE FLOWERING OF HOPE ON THE HEBRON ROAD

On the Hebron Road, heading out of Bethlehem, there is a school called Hope Flowers School. The Founder and Director of the School, Hussein Issa, says, 'We call the school Hope Flowers because the students learn respect for others, and in this way the hope will flower and become a reality.' It aims to be an oasis of hope, where up to 350 students come to the village of Al-Khader (St George) and receive education, including peace and democracy education. The school believes in bringing together Muslim, Christian and Jew and Israeli volunteers come to help teach and learn about Palestinians and, in turn, to let Palestinians meet with Jewish people. I talked first with Hala Hussein Issa, the 24-year-old Deputy Director of the school and daughter of the Principal. She says:

My hope for the future is a life of justice that anyone can have elsewhere in the world. Because here we have no justice, we have no life that can be said to be for human beings. You need a permit to go anywhere. You can't dream or make your dreams come true because of the situation.

For me, my faith is to believe in God and to have faith in freedom and justice. We are Muslims and we have many things we are proud of and many things we believe. Peace is the name of God. God has ninety-nine names and peace is one of them. The Koran itself asks people to be peaceful and to deal with each other in a peaceful way, to respect each other, but many people act against this. To kill anyone with no good reason goes against this. But here many have been killed. Last month there was a bomb in Israel and many innocent women and children were killed, while the Koran itself does not accept the killing of children and women. There are many things done which go against Islam and give a very bad idea about Islam, while it isn't like that.

I get on well with the Christians in the local area... I studied at Bethlehem University and seventy per cent of the students were Christian. I never thought, this one is a Christian or this one a Muslim. There are many Christians who are loving and respect Muslims more than themselves.

We have to make something new. We have to forget some of the things that have happened in the past, so that the future will be much better.

Jewish volunteer Victoria Bush teaches mathematics at the school. She grew up in Poland, in Warsaw, moved to Israel in 1968 and now lives in Jerusalem. I asked her why she came here, and she answered:

It's a way of taking a stand. I guess we all need to express who we are and what we stand for. Israel is lately flooded with ugly religious nationalism and it's my way of expressing that, though I belong here, I don't belong to ugly religious nationalism. I am third generation non-religious. I'm trying to be a tolerant person. I also belong to the Women's Peace Organization which has a considerable percentage of religious women.

One of the problems today is that, for many Israelis, Arabs are mythical beings rather than real human beings. If there were a way of somehow bringing people together, it would make a difference.

Speaking with Hussein Issa, the Founder and Director of Hope Flowers School, I noticed that on the wall of his office there was a Martin Luther King poster with the words, 'From every mountainside let freedom ring.' Hussein had lived in a village called Bayt Far near Ramle until 1948 when, like so many other refugees from that area, they fled across to Bethlehem, where he lived in the Dheisheh Refugee Camp. He says:

After 1967, after we were occupied by Israel, we were in a time of great humiliation. I started thinking about re-educating our people on how our enemies are thinking and working: to know the Hebrew language and the Jewish culture, and to build a new generation, open-minded, to work for peace... We hope and are working to build a new well-educated state. Our experience here is that we have excellent relationships with the three religions—Judaism, Christianity and Islam—and we teach Palestinians about the three religions. We're teaching people about Jewish feasts—Yom Kippur, Hanukkah—and also about Christian feasts like Christmas and Easter. Here in this school, Christians, Muslims and Jews are working together in the same classroom. For the new millennium, I hope for, and I'm looking for, an end to violence and wars; an end to a war every fifty years or every thirty years. It's enough. The human being has become more educated. It feels like we're living in the Middle Ages here. Let us develop economy and agriculture. So, for me, I would destroy all weapons and change weapons like tanks to agricultural tools. Let us put our hands together to divide our bread and have a new education, a new way of health, and get rid of war, and have a new start.

Another Jewish volunteer, Nancy Margelit, who teaches Hebrew language, says:

There is a whole group of Palestinians who want to get to know Israelis and establish a peaceful co-existence. The only way this can happen is through endeavours like Hope Flowers School. We all need to break down the stereotypes and get over the fear and mistrust.

PRAYER
Come, Lord Jesus. Come to us, Lord Jesus Christ; come as we search the scriptures and see God's hidden purpose; come as we walk the lonely road, needing a companion; come when life mystifies and perplexes us; come into our disappointments and our needs; and come in, open our eyes to recognize you.

Donald Hilton, from *Pilgrim to the Holy Land*, McCrimmon

RUTH AND BOAZ ARE MARRIED

RUTH 4:13–17
So Boaz took Ruth and she became his wife. When they came together, the Lord made her conceive, and she bore a son. Then the

women said to Naomi, 'Blessed be the Lord, who has not left you this day without next-of-kin; and may his name be renowned in Israel! He shall be to you a restorer of life and a nourisher of your old age; for your daughter-in-law who loves you, who is more to you than seven sons, has borne him.' Then Naomi took the child and laid him in her bosom, and became his nurse. The women of the neighbourhood gave him a name, saying, 'A son has been born to Naomi.' They named him Obed; he became the father of Jesse, the father of David.

So the story reaches a happy conclusion. Ruth's commitment to Naomi means that Naomi, the empty one, has had her life restored to her. Boaz has done his duty within the customs of his society and has, in some sense, redeemed Ruth. He provides her with an heir for her husband Mahlon (or so it would be viewed), and Ruth provides Naomi with a son. The name is Obed, which means 'servant', and he was the father of Jesse, who in turn was the father of David, who in turn, of course, was an ancestor of Jesus.

In the passage before today's reading, when Boaz has done his deal with the next-of-kin, the people who are witnesses say, 'May the Lord make the woman who is coming into your house like Rachel and Leah, who together built up the house of Israel. May you produce children in Ephrathah and bestow a name in Bethlehem; and, through the children that the Lord will give you by this young woman, may your house be like the house of Perez, who Tamar bore to Judah' (Ruth 4:11–12). This is the only place in the Old Testament where someone is blessed with a wish to be like other women. Certainly Ruth and Boaz 'bestowed a name in Bethlehem' and this beautiful story plays a part in the line of both David and Jesus.

Today if you go down to Beit Sahour, a Christian village just close to Bethlehem, you can look at an area designated as Boaz's field. You catch a glimpse of a rural way of life and agricultural fields a little distance from Bethlehem that help one to visualize the setting of this story. On my recent visit to Beit Sahour and the Bethlehem area, I met Ayman Abu-Zulouf. He's a Christian who has lived in Beit Sahour all his life, and so have his parents. Ayman was a tremendous companion who took us around all sorts of different places in the West Bank as our guide. He has many frustrations at the moment because of the current situation, but nevertheless is trying to pursue his chosen vocation. He trained at Bethlehem Bible College to guide tourist groups. I asked him his hopes for the future and he said:

I hope and pray for a better future, a future where we may be free here—where we can all have freedom of access in my country. Being an indigenous person here, as were my parents, I care about justice and peace and I want them to prevail in this country. Personally I'm fed up with the bloodshed and problems. I want to live a natural life with peace and equality.

To PRAY ABOUT
At the end of this week, let us pray for the coming of the Lord Jesus into various situations. Remember, we started with Mary up at Ein Karem, and the wonderful words from her song. We were reminded of the refugees fleeing from that area, and we end up with the great story of Ruth down in Bethlehem and Beit Sahour. Here again we find the people today who live in Bethlehem and Beit Sahour overwhelmed with the difficulty of their current situation, and so it strengthens the relevance of our prayer, 'Come, Lord Jesus.'

LIGHTING THE CANDLE
Light this week's candle and allow your thoughts to dwell on Mary's song, then to journey from Ein Karem with the refugees to Bethlehem, to find hope with Ruth and Boaz's story, and to pray for those today in Bethlehem and Beit Sahour, that they too will find hope.

Take time now to think of other situations in the world that are on your mind, and then about your own situation and the situations of your family and friends and of your own local church, and bring these needs and hopes to God, praying, 'Come, Lord Jesus.'

BETHLEHEM—THE BEAUTY OF THE LAND
In 1968, the year after the war of '67, the relations between Jews and Palestinians were much less antagonistic than they are today. The whole situation was new and no one knew how long the occupation would last. So as a teenager who was curious and also caught up in some of this reconnecting us with the land, I used to take hikes in the West Bank, and my friends and I would also hike in the hills around

Bethlehem. I got to know many of the springs and many of the terraces, and it was beautiful. The stories I could tell you about Bethlehem or its outskirts and about the nature there—it was wonderful.

Two days ago I was visiting Aida refugee camp and my escort, Omar, stopped to show me a reservoir—he thought it was Turkish but I think it's older than that. For the first time in maybe twenty years I saw the beauty of the land, and I felt I had access to it, but this time with a Palestinian, not as a conquering Israeli Jew, and maybe not so far down the road there is the possibility that we could explore the land together—it could happen.

Rabbi Jeremy Milgrom

ADVENT 3

Voice of the Prophets
Signposts of Hope

Two Kinds Of Bethlehem

Zoughbi Zoughbi

You know, there are two kinds of Bethlehem, as there are two kinds of Jerusalem—heavenly and earthly. When I hear Bethlehem spoken of as city of peace, it's heavenly Bethlehem, because what we are facing in Bethlehem is not peace. We are witnessing pieces of conflict but I feel that instead of cursing darkness we are trying to light a candle for hope—a candle that brings some smiles to people, and it will bring peace, a city of peace. I don't want to have a romantic point of view, but this is the hope that I'm working for, and this is why I would like to have a better future, to make my life and my children's life different from now. It means a lot of dedication, perseverance; it needs the world's support to move this. I feel that spirituality should be part of the reconstruction of Bethlehem.

We hear about Bethlehem 2000. I believe that what is needed now is not only to have good infrastructure but to prepare a room for our Lord Jesus Christ in our heart. If we haven't that room in our heart, I don't think there will be any change. Without this kind of real dynamics, without this chemistry and this vision of peace, this vision of 'house of bread', we're nothing... I believe that where there is a will, there is a way. What is needed is a good number of people committed by their faith, committed to work, committed by their vision, to change the situation.

SUNDAY OF WEEK 3
(Third Sunday of Advent)

The First Sign

ISAIAH 7:13–15

Then Isaiah said: 'Hear then, O house of David! Is it too little for you to weary mortals, that you weary my God also? Therefore the Lord himself will give you a sign. Look, the young woman is with child and shall bear a son, and shall name him Immanuel. He shall eat curds and honey by the time he knows how to refuse the evil and choose the good.'

MATTHEW 1:22–23
All this took place to fulfil what had been spoken by the Lord through the prophet: 'Look, the virgin shall conceive and bear a son, and they shall name him "Emmanuel", which means, "God is with us"'.

This week we are looking at some of the signposts of hope that point us towards Christmas and the birth of a child. We are also looking at signposts of hope from the prophets in terms of pointing to the values and the commitments to justice and wholeness. Our first reading today comes in a passage of Isaiah, where Isaiah is trying to give confidence to King Ahaz, the king of Judah, who is under attack from Syria and Israel. We learn from 2 Kings that King Ahaz is terrified and indeed sacrifices his son to the gods and prepares for armed conflict. He is condemned for this by the author of Kings, so Isaiah's task has been to try to get him to trust in Yahweh and not in war or violence, and Ahaz is encouraged to seek a sign. It is interesting in the light of his action that the nature of the sign he's been given is of a child called 'God with us'. It's perhaps a reminder of the value of the child sacrificed as well as a reminder that there is no need to panic, and that God is beside us.

In this passage, Ahaz is strongly seen as 'of the house of David', and though he is lacking in confidence he is given this sign, for him and for his house, that a woman will bear a son and shall name him Immanuel—'God with us'. This child will seem to have a discipline of hardship, i.e. the curds and honey, that will teach him how to reject evil and choose good. In Matthew's Gospel, this passage is picked up as one of the first of ten occasions where Matthew talks of the scriptures being fulfilled or the words of the prophets being fulfilled. The first time is in a dream that Joseph has, about whether he should break off his relationship with Mary because she's pregnant. In this dream, he is informed that she is a fulfilment of prophecy, and so too her son, Emmanuel, who is a sign that God is with us. This is a theme that goes right through Matthew until the last words, when the disciples are with Jesus and he commissions them to 'go and make disciples of all nations.' Jesus adds, 'Remember, I am with you always, to the end of the age'—a final echo of 'God with us'.

Our Advent journey is a time of waiting and watching, of praying 'Come, Lord Jesus' to different situations—yet with the ultimate knowledge that God is with us, in our lives, in our struggles, in our hopes and in our fears, and that this is the incredible Christmas message.

Every Christmas Eve, I read my favourite poem of John Betjeman, called 'Christmas', which starts with the words, 'The bells of waiting Advent ring'. It paints a wonderful picture of the Christmas of his time, maybe an image of the 1950s, and then it comes to the crunch:

And is it true? And is it true,
This most tremendous tale of all,
Seen in a stained-glass window's hue,
A Baby in an ox's stall?
The Maker of the stars and sea
Become a Child on earth for me?

And is it true? For if it is,
No loving fingers tying strings
Around those tissued fripperies,
The sweet and silly Christmas things,
Bath salts and inexpensive scent
And hideous ties so kindly meant,

No love that in a family dwells,
No carolling in frosty air,
Nor all the steeple-shaking bells
Can with this single Truth compare—
That God was Man in Palestine
And lives today in Bread and Wine.

John Betjeman

The family watch me with some amusement as I read it because they know that I find it very hard to get through it without getting emotionally choked up. To me, the emotions are so strong because Betjeman puts his finger on the key truth: that if this story is true, nothing can compare with the fact that God was with humanity in

Palestine of old, and is with us today in bread and wine, in our daily encounters, and on the journey beside us. This is the message. God is not a distant god, cut off from humanity, but is 'God with us'.

MONDAY OF WEEK 3

A STONE FROM PARADISE

AMOS 5:21–24
I hate, I despise your festivals, and I take no delight in your solemn assemblies. Even though you offer me your burnt offerings... I will not accept them... Take away from me the noise of your songs; I will not listen to the melody of your harps. But let justice roll down like waters, and righteousness like an everflowing stream.

I brought a stone back with me from my visit to the Holy Land in February 1998. I call it a holy stone. Those who know me will be amazed. We run tours that are particularly to meet 'living stones' because the local Christian community feels ignored by so many pilgrims who rush around looking at old stones but won't meet the 'living stones'. But I brought back this stone as a reminder of a painful encounter in a place called Paradise. We were driving out of Bethlehem and had just been up to the hill Jabal abu Ghoneim, where the Israelis are building the Har Homa settlement. This beautiful wooded hill is now savagely scarred with roads and most of the trees have been removed. We then went along the twisty road around the hillsides in this area of Shepherds' Fields, and regularly came upon the sight of families sitting in makeshift tents beside homes that had been demolished. It is from one of these houses that I picked up my stone. Indeed, Ibrahim, the owner, asked me to take it as a reminder of the day the Israeli army arrived without warning and bulldozed it.

As we stood there, overwhelmed by the pain of these families, I looked around. We were very close to the hill Herodian, the cone-shaped hill built by Herod around AD30. To the Arabs it's known as Jabal al-Faradis, the mount of Paradise, and that mount gives the name to this little village of Paradise. Then I turned the other way and saw a village on the hillside, and I asked the name of the village. It was Tekoa, from where the prophet Amos had come. So after saying goodbye to the family, we drove down the road and up to Tekoa. Here we were at the birthplace of Amos, who, according to tradition, is buried here. It's a beautiful area in which to walk, and we were told that there is a huge underground lake in this region that has been there since Amos' time, and this water is pumped away from the local community to Jerusalem and to the settlements. We were reminded of the words, 'Let justice roll on like a river and right living like an everflowing stream', and we thought that the underground waters of Tekoa must have been in Amos' mind as he said these words. We hoped that these waters of justice would flow down to the village of Paradise, flow to the scarred and battered hill of Jabal abu Ghoneim and through the Shepherds' Fields, flow on to Hebron, to Jerusalem, and heal the wounds of the hurting communities—that these waters of justice would bring justice for Palestinian and Jew and make this desperately unholy land a holy place. My stone is a reminder to pray for justice and for the healing of these communities.

Our passage from Amos is in the context of worship. God, through the prophet Amos, is critical of people's religious activities. We will find that this is a common theme in the prophets. God takes no delight in their solemn assemblies or their burnt offerings, he doesn't like their worship songs (this is the only time that music is criticized in the Bible) when worship is performed while ignoring the needs of the poor. Amos, this shepherd of Tekoa, speaks a very strong word from God against those who pursue violence and ignore the sufferings of the poor, and trample them and push aside the needy in the gate.

TO DO

Today, think of the community living so close to Tekoa, Amos' home town—people out on the hillsides, the demolished homes. Pray for them. Pray for justice to flow across that community, and pray for the homeless and forgotten in our own community, and that the waters of justice and healing will flow across our land, for the homeless, for the victims of racism, for the marginalized and forgotten.

TUESDAY OF WEEK 3

SWORDS INTO PLOWSHARES

Micah 4:3–4; 6:8
They shall beat their swords into plowshares, and their spears into pruning hooks; nation shall not lift up sword against nation, neither shall they learn war any more; but they shall all sit under their own vines and under their own fig trees, and no one shall make them afraid; for the mouth of the Lord of hosts has spoken... He has told you, O mortal, what is good; and what does the Lord require of you but to do justice, and to love kindness, and to walk humbly with your God?

Micah, prophesying in the eighth century before Christ, came from Moresheth-Gath, which seems to have been a city from the lower country of south-west Judah, west of Hebron and perhaps not far from Lachish. Not much is known about him, but he is strongly committed to social justice and has a vision of a community that will beat swords into plowshares—a place where nations will no longer need to fight, and each community can sit under its own vines and under its own fig trees without fear. In those days, the Lord will assemble the lame, the afflicted and those that have been driven away (Micah 4:6). So his vision is of a compassionate community which will bring forth a leader from Bethlehem, who will be the one of peace, as we saw on the Tuesday of Week 2.

In chapter 6, Micah gets into a discussion about what God requires and this is very reminiscent of the prophet Amos saying that God hates and despises their feasts and religious activities. Micah asks whether God will be pleased with the sacrifice of thousands of rams and rivers of oil, and then, 'Shall I give my firstborn?' (6:7) We've seen that Ahaz sacrificed his son, and Micah may well have been speaking around the same time as Isaiah and during the reign of Ahaz. Then at the end of this section come those wonderful words: 'He has told you, O mortal, what is good.' We still want all sorts of varied religious activities, but these calming words remind us to do justice, to love kindness, or show mercy, and to walk humbly with God.

It's as if God breathes a sigh at this point, through the prophet, after listing all these different activities that people indulge in to try and win God's favour, and God calls them back to living rightly in a good relationship with neighbour and with God. Micah is another signpost along our way, pointing to the kind of world where the values of God's reign will be dominant, where the weapons of oppression and violence will be rejected, and where people can live in communities at peace with one another and their environment. Many long for this as a 'normal way of life'. Having talked to people in areas such as Hebron, and Bethlehem, and Beit Sahour, I know that they long to be normal, they long to be allowed to sit under their own fig tree.

To build such communities, all of us must make sure there is no oxygen on which violence can feed. We must make sure that attitudes that would lead to one group of people attacking another are not allowed to flourish. Nationalism can often cause this. When I was travelling in Croatia, I could see first-hand amongst the refugees from Bosnia and Croatia the way in which the nationalism of greater Serbia had caused such violence and pain, and we have seen it in other places such as Rwanda. In subtle ways we can feed xenophobia and the sense that we're better than others. The Christian community must be a place which always refuses to let such attitudes flourish, and shows a vision of what the reign of God can and should be like.

So much money is spent on the arms trade. In Britain, making arms is one of the chief sources of employment—and then we react with horror when they're used. Many poorer countries spend ridiculous sums of money on arms when they should be building up the infrastructure in their own community. At present we have India and Pakistan wasting money on nuclear bombs. Israel has stockpiled huge quantities of nuclear weapons at Dimona. Mordechai Vanunu, who was a nuclear technician at the plant, in the end felt compelled to speak out about what was happening. Though a Jew, he has come to Christian faith, and his faith motivated him to speak up. Kidnapped from Europe, he was tried and imprisoned, kept in solitary confinement for eleven years. Now he's out of solitary, but he still languishes in Ashkelon prison, not so far away from where Micah spoke these words, while people campaign for his release.

Two such people are Nick and Mary Eoloff, campaigners against nuclear weapons, who have been so concerned about Vanunu that they officially adopted him in the United States, and they have been to Ashkelon prison to visit him.

We visited him in February 1998 in a very sterile waiting room where we were separated by a steel grill. The visit was very intense and emotionally draining… We were devastated. Mordechai looked much older than his forty-three years but one could sense that his spirit was strong… Then we visited twice with him in March and our first visit was wonderfully uplifting. He looked years younger and shared the joy he felt at being out of solitary. The second visit was rather gloomy as the parole hearing was coming up and he'd been accused of smuggling out an interview with his brother. As a consequence the prison system declared that his brother could not visit him for one year!

MARY AND NICHOLAS EOLOFF— SIGNPOSTS TO PEACE

Mary:
We first got involved with Mordechai because we are anti-nuclear people. We are actually for all disarmament and I read in a magazine in our country that Mordechai was in prison for revealing that Israel had secret nuclear weapons when they were denying it. In addition to that, it said that he was in Ashkelon prison with an 18 years sentence, in a 6 feet by 9 feet cell, so between the horribleness of the punishment and the good deed for which he was being punished, I decided to write to him. I believe we're all one, not only all humanity but all of creation and it's that fundamental spiritual belief that motivates—not everything I do, because I don't always do good things—but what I want to do.

Nicholas:

And for me, nuclear weapons are intrinsically evil and no nation may ever use them, ever, ever, ever, even in defence. So if you can't use them, you can't possess them, and you can't manufacture them. That's where we're coming from.

TO PRAY ABOUT

Pray for Mordechai Vanunu. If he's still in prison, pray for his release and for his state of mind after eleven years in solitary. If he's out, thank God for his witness and pray for him as he adjusts. Also pray for all who, like Mordechai, are prisoners of conscience. Thank God for the witness of people like Nick and Mary Eoloff and their determination that we should beat our swords into plowshares. Find out more about the arms trade in Britain and the impact that it has on countries around the world, where people become victims of the success of this trade. CAAT, the Campaign Against the Arms Trade, is a good place to start to gain information. Their address is 11 Goodwin Street, London N4 3HQ. Tel: 0171-281 0297; Fax: 0171-281 4369; e-mail: caat@gn.apc.org.

PRAYER

Lord, in this time of Advent, we thank you for the signpost of Micah. Forgive us for believing in the myth of redemptive violence, for believing that weapons can bring peace. Instead, may we be those who follow in your footsteps by doing justice, showing mercy, and walking humbly with you. Help us to create communities of peace, that are a witness to your alternative values and to your reign. Amen

TERRORIST

No one can catch you—you cover your tracks
While your dirty work's done in East Timor and Iraq
Your fingerprints are on guns the whole world over
In El Salvador, Somalia, the Middle East and Cambodia
You've got blood on your hands.

'In the interests of security' you sell weapons to all nations
Fuelling the genocide of indigenous populations

The fact is your interests are purely economic
You enslave a people to increase your profit
You've got blood on your hands

Spin doctored speeches image and news
Leaves the search for the terrorist somewhat confused
As you point the finger at Palestinian and Iraqi
Underneath your shirt sleeves what's that I see—
                              blood on your hands?!

Your imperialist crusade will not be contained
'Coercive diplomacy' as you like it named
We won't be fooled by your bullshit and lies
It's a reign of terror you legitimise
You've got blood on your hands

Jonny Baker and Jon Birch, Proost Publishing, 1998

WEDNESDAY OF WEEK 3

TRUE FASTING

ISAIAH 58:3–8

Look, you serve your own interest on your fast day, and oppress all your workers… Such fasting as you do today will not make your voice heard on high… Will you call this a fast, a day acceptable to the Lord? Is not this the fast that I choose: to loose the bonds of injustice, to undo the thongs of the yoke, to let the oppressed go free, and to break every yoke? Is it not to share your bread with the hungry, and bring the homeless poor into your house; when you see the naked, to cover them, and not to hide yourself from your own kin? Then your light shall break forth like the dawn, and your healing shall spring up quickly.

Once again, this is a passage where one of the prophets tackles the issue of what is true religion, what is true spirituality and what is acceptable worship to God. Here we have people fasting and yet they are apparently arguing in the middle of their fasts. They are not humbling themselves, and in particular they are not doing those things which are acceptable to God, that is, looking after the poor and letting the oppressed go free. It is interesting that when Jesus reads a passage from Isaiah in the synagogue, although it's predominantly from Isaiah 61, he includes some words from this chapter (v. 6)—to 'let the oppressed go free'. Jesus was obviously steeped in Isaiah, not only the image of the suffering servant, but also the commitment to this way of life that brings good news to the poor and breaks the bonds of injustice.

It is consistency of life that is being called for here in Isaiah, just as it was in Amos and Micah. This is later picked up in the letter of James in the New Testament. Unless we live out our worship and our understanding of God and put faith into action, it is not true worship. Sharing bread with the hungry is a tremendous challenge when we consider how many go to bed each night hungry in our world. Looking after the homeless poor, in a world of refugees and homelessness, is another huge challenge.

I had a friend called Misaeri Kauma. He was Bishop of Namirembe in Uganda for many years, then retired and, sadly, in 1997 died rather unexpectedly. But he was a person of cheerful, warm faith who was always committed to showing love in action, and I remember that at one time he and his wife Geraldine had over eighty refugees in their home up in Namirembe, during one of the times of conflict within Uganda. In his retirement he became president of the Uganda AIDS commission and formed his own little charity with AIDS Orphans in his own community of Nakatema Nsangi—a project which is now called the Taata project (which means 'Dad') in memory of Misaeri. His life was an act of worship because faith and action were so interlinked and, therefore, an enormous challenge and motivation to me and to many others.

People who stand up against injustice are often awkward characters. They keep raising the points that we'd rather not hear; they keep rocking the boat, whereas it's quieter if you preserve the equilibrium and the *status quo*. But, of course, they have understood what it is to be a true follower of God, what it is to live the values of the reign of God, and what it is to be a true worshipper. Faith and worship are not just to keep us personally comfortable, they are to remind us how to serve God by serving our neighbour. As I have already mentioned, my son, Tom, worked for several years for the project down in East London in South Africa called Isaiah 58. The project took street kids off the streets and brought them into a home, where they were given accommodation, education, health care and a good, hopeful Christian upbringing. The local Christians had called the project 'Isaiah 58' because they were looking after the homeless poor, the most vulnerable young ones, and giving them the possibility of a life with some hope. It's interesting that this passage ends with a promise, that if we do these things, 'Your light shall rise in the darkness'. We create a better world, which is for the benefit of all of us, if we walk this way.

PRAYER
Ruler of the everlasting kingdom, prince of peace, champion of the despised: you are the King; you make a cross your throne; you wear a crown of thorns; you call your subjects friends. Help us to take up our cross, to hunger and thirst for all that is good; then will your kingdom come on earth as in heaven. Amen
New Zealand Prayer Book

THURSDAY OF WEEK 3

THE FEAST OF LIFE

Isaiah 40:3–5, 11
A voice cries out: 'In the wilderness prepare the way of the Lord, make straight in the desert a highway for our God. Every valley shall be lifted up, and every mountain and hill be made low; the uneven ground shall become level, and the rough places a plain. Then the glory of the Lord shall be revealed and all people shall see it together... He will feed his flock like a shepherd; he will gather the lambs in his arms, and carry them in his bosom, and gently lead the mother sheep.'

These words from Isaiah 40 are echoed or directly quoted in the earliest passages of the Gospels, in Mark, Matthew and Luke. Luke quotes right through to the passage about, 'Every valley shall be filled, and every mountain and hill shall be made low' (see Luke 3:4–6). So the Gospel writers saw a tremendous fulfilment of this chapter in John the Baptist's role of preparing the way for Jesus and for the values of a reign where injustices in society would be rejected. This prepares the way for God's kingdom. When we think of Mary's prophetic words at Ein Karem, the same issues are reflected: the powerful will be brought down, and the low will be lifted up, and the hungry will be filled with good things, and the rich sent empty away. Today's passage reflects a society that moves towards these healing values.

The signposts of the prophets are undoubtedly signposts of hope as they point to a new world with new values, where we see the character of God as not only strong, but also compassionate and tender. In verse 11, 'He will feed his flock like a shepherd; he will gather the lambs in his arms, and carry them in his bosom, and gently lead the mother sheep.' This is the one who is our strength and our guide, but who has a tenderness and a sensitivity that reflect the character of the God who desires that 'the uneven ground shall become level'.

Just before I joined Christian Aid in 1996, I came across their 50th birthday statement of faith and commitment called 'All Shall Be Included… In The Feast Of Life'. Since then I've written a musical picking up this theme. The statement inspired me because it seems to reflect the justice and the compassion that these words from Isaiah point towards.

We believe that God hopes and works for a world where all shall be included in the feast of life and that in Christ we see how costly it is to bring that world about.

We believe that God's strategy for a new world is to put the poorest first and that nothing is more important for God's people than to bring the poor good news.

We believe the rich and poor alike can be generous, wise and creative because all are made in God's image and that all are made poorer when any are left out.

We confess that we use our strength to protect ourselves and order the world to benefit the rich and not the poor and that none of us can be trusted with too much power over others.

We believe that loving our neighbours means working for justice so that all have a say in what happens to them.

We believe that God made the good earth to sustain and delight us and that we are called to take care of it and enjoy it.

We believe that the God of all the earth is at work beyond the churches as well as within them making common cause with all who want the poor to be included.

We long for the time when the meek shall inherit the earth and all who hunger and thirst after justice shall be satisfied and we believe that, despite the persistence of evil, now is always the time when more good can be done and we can make a difference.

These words remind me that it is the little acts that all of us can do that can reflect these values of the reign of God. Simple acts like reminding our supermarkets to have ethical standards regarding the treatment of those who grow or pack the food around the world that ends up on their shelves. Simple acts like writing letters when we know that something is wrong in our world or that someone is being ignored or is the victim of injustice, to let a government know that they're being watched. Grass will wither and the flower will fade, powerful nations will come and go—so will powerful leaders—but these words of the Lord will endure because they're words of lasting resonance and relevance for every generation as he leads us gently to a world of compassionate values.

PRAYER
Come humbly, holy child,
Stir in the womb
Of our complacency;
Shepherd our vision
Of the little we need
For abundant living.
  Come humbly, holy spirit,
To whisper through the leaves

In the garden of our ignorance,
Exposing our blindness
To children dying,
Hungry and in pain.
    Come humbly, holy light,
Pierce our lack of generosity and love,
Scattering our dark fear
Of living freely in your way,
Poured out in wanton service.
    Come humbly, holy wisdom,
Cry through the empty streets
Of our pretence to care,
That the face of the poor
Will be lifted up,
For holy is your name.
    Come humbly, holy God,
Be born into our rejoicing,
Come quickly, humble God,
And reign.

G.K., from a Mothers' Union day on the Magnificat, Durham 1989

FRIDAY OF WEEK 3

DO THEY FEEL MY SHADOW?
(JUBILEE HOPES FROM BETHLEHEM)

ISAIAH: 61:1–3

The spirit of the Lord God is upon me, because the Lord has anointed me; he has sent me to bring good news to the oppressed, to bind up the brokenhearted, to proclaim liberty to the captives, and release to the prisoners; to proclaim the year of the Lord's favour, and the day of vengeance of our God; to comfort all who mourn; to provide for those who mourn in Zion—to give them a garland instead of ashes, the oil of gladness instead of mourning, the mantle of praise instead of a faint spirit.

As we have already seen, this is the passage Jesus uses when he first defines his ministry (Luke 4:18–19), though he slightly changes it and adds a line from Isaiah 58. It is also interesting to note what he leaves out. He does not include the line 'and the day of vengeance of our God'. He defines his ministry in terms of healing and restoring, bringing liberation and proclaiming a permanent year of jubilee, which seems to be the reference of 'proclaiming the year of the Lord's favour' (Isaiah 61:2). Jesus seems to be suggesting that this extraordinary jubilee has arrived, when all the land reverts back to the creator, who distributes it equally and with generosity.

The jubilee concept was a poignant one to the Palestinian community as Israel arrived at its fiftieth anniversary as a state in 1998. In 1948 the Palestinians had their land taken forcibly and 418 villages destroyed, with three-quarters of a million people turned into refugees and made homeless. It is not surprising that many talked of jubilee and what it would mean in this context. In Bethlehem, the Sabeel Liberation Theology group held a conference at Bethlehem University on the theme of 'The Challenge of Jubilee—what does God require?' More than nine hundred people, both local and international, came to the conference to try to discern God's call for them to be peacemakers, promoting justice for all people, and to stand in solidarity with the local people and proclaim the challenge of jubilee. Palestinians remember al-Nakba (the catastrophe) and in this conference many passages from the Bible were looked at, including Leviticus 25:10, which talks of proclaiming liberty to all the land's inhabitants.

At the end, Sabeel issued this statement:

The challenge is to practise perpetual jubilee and to articulate a new vision for peace, justice and security, and coexistence that satisfies the deepest needs of all God's people, rather than a solution based on military might and on a 'balance of power' which inevitably favours the strong and allows for racism, oppression and discrimination against the weak... The benefits of God's jubilee are for all the inhabitants of this land, Israelis and Palestinians, Muslims, Jews and Christian. The promise fulfilled will be for a life of true peace with lasting security for all people of the region.

At that time, I also visited my friend, Bishara Awad, Director of Bethlehem Bible College, and asked him about the prophets as signposts of hope. He talked of the need for real prophets:

I love all the prophets of the Old Testament. I have read the Old Testament, we teach the Old Testament here at Bethlehem Bible College, and the prophets have a clear message. It is a message of salvation and redemption. The prophets have called the people back to God. I like the later prophets, where they talk about justice—Amos, for example. He lived right here in Tekoa, which is right next to Bethlehem, so he's our neighbour. But truly these days what we need is a real prophet and not all of these false prophets who dwell only on prophecies and promises that have already been fulfilled over and over. We need true prophets of God that can clearly talk against injustices, and that will ask people to return to God. With the coming of Jesus—Jesus loved the whole world—there is no person who is better than another person any more. Maybe in the Old Testament we may have a chosen people through whom God worked. The reason he worked with them was so that they would be a light to all nations. Then Jesus came, and said, 'You are the light of the world.' We Christians, who believe in Jesus and have accepted Jesus as our Saviour, we are the light, and we are the true light here in Bethlehem. The Bethlehem Bible College is light to the whole community here and we believe that we are his people like the Bible says.

Here in Bethlehem we live among Muslims and Christians and we have been living as good neighbours with the Muslim Palestinians. We reach out to people in love. For example, there are three refugee camps that are very close to us here. We give them food and clothing. We send medical teams to them, or coaches to help them with sports, and English teachers. In fact, a few years ago, they wrote a big sign right in front of one of the camps, which is one hundred percent Muslim, which said, 'We appreciate the work of Bethlehem Bible College,' so we are making an impact, a Christian impact, to the whole community. This is where we wanted to be, to show the love of Christ to everybody.

Poem
I walk between
Darkness and light
The night of exile and

The morning memory of home
The land I knew
Is given up to strangers
There is no sunshine
Do they feel my shadow?

Anon

PRAYER

God our Father, you spoke to the prophets of old of a Saviour who would bring peace. You helped them to spread the joyful message of his coming kingdom. Help us, as we prepare to celebrate his birth, to share with those around us the good news of your power and love. We ask this through Jesus Christ, the Light who is coming into the world.

From *The Promise Of His Glory*, Church House Publishing,

© St George's, Oakdale

SATURDAY OF WEEK 3

TWO SARIS AND A BUCKET

PHILIPPIANS 2:3–11

Do nothing from selfish ambition or conceit, but in humility regard others as better than yourselves. Let each of you look not to your own interests, but to the interests of others. Let the same mind be in you that was in Christ Jesus, who, though he was in the form of God, did not regard equality with God as something to be exploited, but emptied himself, taking the form of a slave, being born in human likeness. And being found in human form, he humbled himself and became obedient to the point of death—even death on a cross. Therefore God also highly exalted him and gave him the name that is above every name, so that at the name of Jesus every knee should bend, in heaven and on earth and under the earth, and every tongue should confess that Jesus Christ is Lord, to the glory of God the Father.

We have spent this week looking at the signposts of the prophets: the first Isaiah, the second Isaiah who was operating a couple of hundred years later, Amos and Micah. Their message has been remarkably similar and, when the Gospel writers look back—particularly Matthew—they see the fulfilment of the promised reign of God in Jesus Christ. Jesus sees it this way, and sees himself in some sense as a successor to the suffering servant who is reflected in the servant songs of Isaiah. Now, as we look at this passage from Philippians, we see how Paul picks out some of the same themes and how this should reflect on the way we live.

First he calls us to reject the selfish way and to follow the way of humility, not to think of ourselves more highly than we should, but to put others first. Then he says that we are to have the same mind that was in Jesus Christ, who refused to exploit his position of equality with God, who took the form of a servant and became God with us in human form, and identified with us in our suffering right to the point of the cross. Paul is pointing out that Jesus refused to exploit power by domination but showed us the ultimate example by humility and service. It is thought that in verses 6–11 Paul is quoting from a hymn that was used by the very earliest Church, perhaps originally written in Aramaic, and this could therefore be one of the oldest passages of the New Testament.

If this is the way of Christ, what is the example that, as Christians, we should be following? This passage makes it very clear. It is one of selflessness and giving ourselves for others. What, therefore, would be success in the Christian life? Jim Wallis, in his book *Agenda for Biblical People* (SPCK, 1984), says:

The gospel knows nothing of what sociologists call 'upward mobility'. In fact, the gospel of Jesus Christ calls us to the reverse; the gospel calls us to a downward pilgrimage. Former attachments and securities in the false values of wealth and power are left behind as we are empowered by the Holy Spirit to seek first the Kingdom.

Basil the Great said:

The bread which you do not use is the bread of the hungry; the garment hanging in the wardrobe is the garment of the one who is naked; the shoes you do not wear are the shoes of the one who is barefoot; the money you keep locked away is the money of the poor; the acts of charity you do not perform are so many injustices that you commit.

From *Common Wealth And Common Good*, Bishop's Conference for Justice, Development and Peace, Collins, 1991

To me the most striking example of success was what Mother Teresa left when she died—two saris and a bucket. She gave away everything and gave her life in service of others. There have been those who have criticized her for not being political enough, and not dealing with the root causes of poverty. But I feel that one can hardly criticize unless one is living with the same level of commitment, and people have different vocations. I had the opportunity to meet her on one occasion and I was going to sing a song to her that I had written, based on some words of hers. She wanted me to sing it to the sisters, but unfortunately they had just taken a vow of silence. For a moment she seemed to hesitate, as if weighing up whether she should allow me to sing the song or not, and I had this awful thought that here I was, tempting Mother Teresa! However, she decided against it and chatted about her work for a while in terms of seeking to bring dignity to the poor because each one is made in the image of God. As we left, I gave her a cassette of the song. As we walked away, my friend, Vijayan Pavenmani, who was a friend of Mother Teresa, chuckled and said, 'If she had a cassette player, she would have given it away and she will have given your cassette away by the end of the day.' He was proved right. No cassette was found with her possessions. There were just two saris and a bucket! But what success, that our lives should be so lived that, at the end, all the resources God has given us have been used up—we've got rid of the excess. We've not looked to our own interests, but we've been humble, emptied ourselves, and followed the way of Christ.

TO THINK ABOUT

In the highly stressful, busy, materialistic world in which we live, a more simple lifestyle where we rid ourselves of some of the possessions that require such hard-working and busy lives to maintain may be liberating, both to ourselves and to others. Advent is a time of penitence and a time of review. If success were to be described as leaving two saris and a bucket, how well would we do?

LIGHTING THE CANDLE

Look back over this week as you light your candle. Light it for the homeless families in Paradise, for Mordechai Vanunu and Nick and Mary Eoloff. Pray that swords will be turned into plowshares and that people won't have to make their living through creating weapons of destruction. Thank God for those who have been the prophetic figures, either people you have read about this week or people you have known in your own life, who have been an example to you. Pray for the witness of Bethlehem Bible College and for Sabeel Liberation Theology Centre, and thank God for the extraordinary example of simplicity from Mother Teresa. Pray that we will both read the signs and be signs.

ADVENT 4 — CHRISTMAS 1

From Darkness to Light

He became poor that we might discover our worth
He became flesh of our flesh to dignify our humanity
At the stable door our lives are changed and we bow in humility
As we find God, utterly vulnerable, yet turning the world
upside down

Garth Hewitt

When God wants an important thing done in this world or a wrong righted, he goes about it in a very singular way. He doesn't release thunderbolts or stir up earthquakes. God simply has a tiny baby born, perhaps of a very humble home, perhaps of a very humble mother. And God puts the idea or purpose into the mother's heart. And she puts it in the baby's mind, and then—God waits. The great events of this world are not battles and elections and earthquakes and thunderbolts. The great events are babies, for each child comes with the message that God is not yet discouraged with humanity, but is still expecting goodwill to become incarnate in each human life.

Edmond McDonald, quoted in *Guide My Feet* by Marian Wright Edelman, Beacon Press

SUNDAY OF WEEK 4
(Fourth Sunday of Advent)

FOUR WOMEN IN JESUS' ANCESTRY

MATTHEW 1:1–2, 5–6, 16–17

An account of the genealogy of Jesus the Messiah, the son of David, the son of Abraham. Abraham was the father of Isaac, and Isaac the father of Jacob, and Jacob the father of Judah and his brothers, and Judah the father of Perez and Zerah by Tamar... and Salmon the father of Boaz by Rahab, and Boaz the father of Obed by Ruth, and Obed the father of Jesse, and Jesse the father of King David. And David was the father of Solomon by the wife of Uriah... and Jacob the father of Joseph the husband of Mary, of whom Jesus was born, who is called the Messiah. So all the generations from Abraham to David are fourteen generations; and from David to the deportation to Babylon, fourteen generations; and from the deportation to Babylon to the Messiah, fourteen generations.

To begin a book with a genealogy would be a turn-off for us, but it is the Near Eastern way of beginning a book. It gives the history of Jesus while saying that if you want to understand Jesus then you need to look back in the Old Testament to see his roots. Jesus is traced back not only to Abraham but also to David. But *en route* there are four fascinating women who are included—Tamar, Rahab, Ruth and Bathsheba, who is referred to as the wife of Uriah.

Luke also has a genealogy of Jesus, which sometimes coincides with Matthew's and sometimes does not (see Luke 3:23–38). One of the key differences is that Luke does not mention any of the women. He traces Jesus again through Joseph's line—'He was the son (as was thought) of Joseph...'—back through his being the son of David and Abraham right through to being the 'son of Adam, son of God'. So Luke again is trying to put Jesus' context in history and both Luke and Matthew are trying to prove his identity in a way that would have been common in Near Eastern writing. It is not so much a literal account as an attempt to authenticate the lineage of someone who might be a king or a priest or a significant figure.

Luke is normally more sympathetic to women in his Gospel, so it is intriguing to find that it is Matthew who has brought in the four women and, indeed, he mentions Mary as well. What is he trying to say? Well, on the one hand, one could say that several of these women had acted in unorthodox ways and might perhaps be treated without respect, and yet they are seen to reflect God's unusual working, which is also seen in the choosing of Mary to be the mother of Christ. Tamar, in Genesis 38, pretends to be a temple prostitute in order to sleep with her father-in-law, and it is not clear from the text whether she was a Canaanite or an Adullamite. She eventually gives birth to twins, who struggle with each other even from the womb, in a similar way to Esau and Jacob. One of these twins, Perez, is shown in Ruth 4 to be an ancestor of David. Equally, both Tamar and Ruth are seen as ancestors of David and, therefore, as ancestors of Jesus.

The next woman in Matthew's genealogy is Rahab, the prostitute, with whom the spies in Joshua 2 spend the night. She is seen as virtuous for having given them shelter and at the end of Joshua she and her family are saved whilst everyone else is killed. She and Salmon are the parents of Boaz, who marries Ruth. So Rahab was certainly not an Israelite, and Tamar was probably not either. Then we come to Ruth, who also was not—she was a Moabite—and Bathsheba, who was the wife of Uriah the Hittite, though it is not clear whether she herself was a Hittite. What is clear is the remarkable inclusiveness of this list. These women are seen to have played a part in God's plan despite decidedly unorthodox relationships in several cases. Again, in several cases, they were from outside the Jewish community and yet played a key part in the genealogy of David and of Jesus. Matthew wrote this in around AD80. Was he at pains to show these unorthodox women in David's line, in order to deal with some people who thought Mary was unorthodox? Indeed, maybe some did not believe that it was a virgin birth, and perhaps Matthew was hinting that, whatever they thought, it was clearly in the plan of God. Who knows? Certainly Matthew was asserting the value and significance of five different women by the end of this genealogy. It may have been the other way round, that because the birth of each of these women's sons had been in some sense irregular, this was preparing people for the irregularity of Jesus' birth, namely Mary's virginity.

What is most heartening about the genealogies is the character of the people involved. Though many of them are heroes of the Bible, one has to say that their characters are exactly like ours—some were good, some not so good, and some were people with very obvious weaknesses who had to struggle both with faith and with life. There is something extremely down-to-earth about all of these characters, and yet Jesus came from them, ordinary people whom God was able to use. This is encouraging for us because it reminds us that Jesus was born into the middle of everyday life, and can be born in us in the middle of everyday life. If we look at the story of the women in the genealogy, or indeed the men, many of them had lives that were in many ways messed up, and yet God was able to bring good out of these situations. God's mercy and encouragement goes on, despite the wrong things we do and the messes that we get into. The four women of the genealogy give us great hope that God lives with us, whoever we are, and that goodness and healing and hope can come out of all sorts of difficult situations.

To DO
Think today of the most hopeless situation that you or one of your friends or relatives are currently faced with. Consider honestly whether it seems more helpless or more of a mess or more hopeless than the situation of Tamar, Ruth, Rahab or Bathsheba. Then bring the situation to God, being encouraged that God's design and wholeness can come into situations that are so difficult.

Prayer
God our Mother, you cradled salvation in a woman's womb, surrounding him with rich warmth in that still darkness, and through history and the women of the genealogy you brought hope out of despair and design out of apparent disorder. Encourage us with that vision in the muddle of everyday life—as you work with us to bring hope and meaning out of the most difficult of circumstances. Amen

J. Massyngbaerde Ford, *Days of the Spirit.* Additional words: Garth Hewitt

MONDAY OF WEEK 4

ZECHARIAH PROPHESIES

LUKE 1:67–69, 76–79
Then... Zechariah was filled with the Holy Spirit and spoke this prophecy: 'Blessed be the Lord God of Israel, for he has looked favourably on his people and redeemed them. He has raised up a mighty saviour for us in the house of his servant David... And you, child, will be called the prophet of the Most High; for you will go before the Lord to prepare his ways, to give knowledge of salvation to his people by the forgiveness of their sins. By the tender mercy of our God, the dawn from on high will break upon us, to give light to those who sit in darkness and in the shadow of death, to guide our feet into the way of peace.'

These beautiful words are part of Zechariah's prophecy when John the Baptist is born. The story has been resonant with Old Testament references because Zechariah, who came from the priestly order and was a descendent of Aaron, and his wife Elizabeth were 'getting on in years'—reminiscent of Abraham and Sarah. Yet Elizabeth became pregnant and Zechariah had been prepared for this by a visit of an angel, just as Mary was to receive a visit from an angel soon afterwards. Zechariah had been struck speechless after receiving the vision and it was only when he wrote on a tablet that the name of the child was not to be Zechariah, but John, that he was able to speak again. Just before today's passage we read that people were pondering, '"What then will this child become?" For, indeed, the hand of the Lord was with him' (1:66).

Now we start to see the nature of John the Baptist in this prophecy. Zechariah roots him in the community of Israel and in the journey of salvation, but verses 76 and 77 show a very special task because he will go before the Lord to prepare his ways. The Benedictus, as this is sometimes called, is probably a pre-Lukan canticle which Luke adapts. There is the suggestion, as we compare this to other parts of Luke's Gospel, that God defeats enemies and effects salvation by bringing people to peace. When John's ministry starts in chapter 3 of Luke, Luke quotes from the prophet Isaiah and describes John as 'the voice of one crying out in the wilderness: Prepare the way of the Lord, make his paths straight. Every valley shall be filled, and every mountain and hill shall be made low.' John is seen as the last of the Old Testament prophets, pointing clearly to the coming of Jesus, who inaugurates the new reign with new values that will turn the values of our world upside-down.

As we come close to Christmas, it's important to think of the alternative values that are reflected in this message. In the middle of the commercialism and the business, there is a simple gospel that brings light and points us to peace. Take time today to get away and be quiet and to pray. John's message was for people to change, to repent, and to be baptized, to get ready for the coming of Jesus. Are there things in our lives that need to change as we get ready to welcome Jesus, at this time of Christmas? Are there things in our lives that need to be turned the right way up? Are there dark places that need some light to be shed, that need to be opened up to the light and the love of God?

ADVENT—WHEN CHRIST MUST BE BORN IN OUR SOULS

We live always during Advent. We are always waiting for the Messiah to come. The Messiah has come, but it's not yet fully manifest. The Messiah is not fully manifest in each of our souls, not fully manifest in human kind as a whole: that is to say, that just as Christ was born according to the flesh in Bethlehem of Judah, so must he be born according to the Spirit in each of our souls.

Jean Danielou

PRAYER
I am the Lord your God.
I have waited on you,
And have heard your prayer.

Now is the right time,
And I am coming soon.

So, prepare a way in the desert,
A cradle in the hay,
A meeting place in the market place,
A table in an upstairs room,
A cross on a hill,
A grave in a garden,
A throne in your heart as in heaven.

For now again,
I will bend down and remember you.

I will answer your prayer,
And your waiting in joy.

From 'Waiting' in *Cloth for the Cradle*, Wild Goose Worship Group

BETHLEHEM 2000

Bethlehem heralded an eternal message to the world: peace on earth and goodwill towards humankind. Let the year 2000 be a transition for the

realization of the dream of all people—peace, love and fraternity everywhere on earth.

President Yasser Arafat

An interview with Rajai Khouri

I talked with architect Rajai Khouri about Bethlehem 2000, not just the events at the turn of the millennium but also about the major Bethlehem 2000 projects, which will take seven years to complete. It is hoped that it will create employment opportunities for the Palestinian community, to encourage private sector investment, to encourage the upgrading and expanding of services—for example, roads and utilities—to improve the living conditions and to encourage the revival of Palestinian culture and heritage. There will be many special events between December 1999 and April 2001, with many Christian activities by the wide range of Christian churches. There will also be folklore, street theatre, music, art exhibitions, guided walks and symposiums. Rajai said:

The whole idea of the project of Bethlehem 2000 is that we expect between two million and three million pilgrims and visitors to come to Bethlehem during the millennium period. What happens today? People go to Bethlehem only for twenty or thirty minutes. The main essence of Bethlehem 2000 is to encourage them to remain in Bethlehem for three days, to create enough interest for the pilgrim to sleep, stay, eat and talk in Bethlehem for three days, and this is the basis of the Bethlehem 2000 construction.

Rajai was born in Jerusalem. When he was one year old, his parents left Jerusalem for Lebanon, expecting to come back soon after, but in the end he did not return to Jerusalem until 1994. He studied at the American University of Beirut and started his business as an architect in the Gulf area. Since 1993 he has been working with the Palestinian Authority in Jerusalem and the Palestinian Territories. He is an optimist and he believes:

This peace is everlasting. Unfortunately we had a setback, but in the interest of everyone, the peace process should go on. We have made a decision that we want to have peace with the Israelis and the Jews, we want to continue hand-in-hand until we get this peace process on its way. Don't forget that my name is Rajai, which means 'hope'. Rhaa is 'hope' and Rhajai is 'my hope' in Arabic, so hope is always there for me.

Rajai sings opera and has a beautiful voice. I first met him when he sang at the consecration of Bishop Riah Abu El-Assal in Jerusalem in 1996. He is an Anglican and lives now in London and worships at St Marylebone Parish Church. I asked him what Christmas means to him.

I look forward to the Christmas season every year. As a Christian, it means a lot to me. Nothing can beat the music of Christmas. I believe the Christmas season is the season for hope, both Advent and Christmas. I have a tradition that I get all my friends together to sing carols. For myself and my children and my family, this is something we'd like to keep on doing—it brings a kind of hope. Then after Christmas, between Christmas and the New Year, this is the time when I prefer to remain at home and think about what is happening, what has happened the previous year, and what is going to happen next year. I always do that, reviewing the past and thinking of the future.

TUESDAY OF WEEK 4

A Light to the Nations

Isaiah 42:1, 3–4
Here is my servant, whom I uphold, my chosen, in whom my soul delights; I have put my spirit upon him; he will bring forth justice to the nations... A bruised reed he will not break, and a dimly burning wick he will not quench; he will faithfully bring forth justice. He will not grow faint or be crushed until he has established justice in the earth.

The coming of the light is drawing closer, the gentle servant will come, who doesn't crush people or break them—'a dimly burning wick he will not quench'—and he will bring forth justice, and he will be a light to our world, to open people's eyes on how to live, and to liberate people from their oppression and to create a community that stretches around the world, that carries on this task and incarnates this reality.

Isaiah says that, in the end, what Advent is really about is the creation of a new world in which there will be only one centre, one people, one light and one reason to be... The prominent Christmas message, however, the one that glitters from billboards and oozes out of Christmas advertising and seduces all the lines of children that troop to Santa Claus, is hardly that I must keep my eye out for the coming of the Christ. No, the ads want me to keep my eye on me. I'm to spend the season deciding what things I'll give and hinting at what things I'd like to get. I'm to forget about what I need to be so that the Reign of God can come, world unity can be and the light can shine for everyone. The ads are wrong, Matthew says, we have to learn to keep alert. We have to learn not to get immersed in the kind of tinny dailiness that numbs our souls, deadens our spirits, deafens our ears to the word... Indeed the questions for Advent are: How is God trying to come into my life right now? ... What should I be doing differently?

Sister Joan Chittister in *Simplify and Celebrate*, Northstone Publishing, 1997

On one Orthodox Christmas Eve (6 January) I visited the Church of the Nativity in Bethlehem along with a group who had come especially for the consecration of Bishop Riah abu-El Assal as the new Anglican Bishop of Jerusalem. Amongst that group was Bishop Leo Frade and his wife Diana from Honduras. Bishop Leo is the Episcopal Bishop of Honduras and his is the fastest growing Episcopal Church in the Americas. They suffered tremendously under the impact of Hurricane Mitch, but they are now rebuilding their lives and community. I asked him whether there was anything special that they did at Christmas to prepare for the coming of Jesus, and he told me about *la Posada*. This is a custom which happens in Honduras in the Episcopal (Anglican) or Catholic churches—it is part of the Spanish tradition and it is done throughout Latin America.

A VOICE FROM HONDURAS

The Posada means 'shelter' or 'inn' and people prepare for Christmas in the seven days before by visiting houses and singing outside them with special Christmas carols. It is to remind people of when Joseph and Mary came looking for a place to stay. However, Leo and Diana pointed out that it's different from carol singing in the States or in Europe because the people in the house deny you entry so you keep on singing, and they keep saying, 'There's no room, there's no room.' It's done several times, and finally they will say, 'Come in' and then there's more singing inside and they offer you coffee and cookies. The songs are special ones that relate to the journey of Mary and Joseph and they talk of their travel and how they are weary and looking for a place to stay. Every night people go out to a different place. Everything has to be planned beforehand because, as Bishop Leo points out, 'If they say "come in" straight away, you blow it! They need to deny entry several times.

'In a way, it's an acted parable that is both fun and significant. Children dress up as Joseph and Mary and the whole thing speaks to the community, and to many who don't come to church.'

Bishop Leo says that the message of this, and the message of Advent that we are communicating, is, 'Let's make sure we have room for Jesus—get ready for Jesus and make sure, when he knocks on our door, we have room for him.'

Another custom in Honduras is the creation of cribs. During Advent people go from house to house to see the different cribs. In the cathedral, half the church becomes a nativity scene and it's a combination of the modern with the old. There will be extra figures there, maybe soldiers or ladies making tortillas—they buy clay models. Then in the corner there will be the traditional scene of Mary and Joseph, animals and the shepherds. The display is so big that it's like a city; indeed, it's modelled on the city of San Pedro Sula where Bishop Leo and Diana live, and there are even streets and cars and bridges and running water. It's fun and a community event for everyone, and everyone brings different pieces.

Their homes are also turned into cribs, and both in their homes and in the cathedral, there are three kings and a camel who start from far away on Christmas Day and gradually start to come closer until 6 January. There is also a tradition of stealing the baby Jesus from the crib. This is the Orthodox influence, reminding people that Christmas should be celebrated on 6 January, and so you may lose the baby from your crib scene, but the baby will re-emerge on 6 January!

Although it's now changing, Christmas Day was not the gift time in Honduras—it was 6 January, to remember when the three kings brought their gifts. That's still the case, though these days it tends to be money and sweets that are put in the stocking on 6 January because the Santa Claus tradition has come down strongly from the States and so children want some presents at Christmas! But when Leo was growing up, they would wait until Epiphany for their gifts.

Las Posadas is the time to open the doors of our hearts to give shelter. How do we give shelter to Jesus? By the doing of good works. It is the preparation time for the doing and practising of the virtues. It is a time for coming together with our neighbours. It is the occasion for gathering with our families and with those who live near us.

Fiestas Navidenas

POSADA PRAYER

Divine and Eternal Word, who descended from the Father into the heart of the Virgin Mary, your love for humankind leads you to Bethlehem where you were born at midnight into a poor and humble stable. In truth, thousands of angels accompany you on this journey, and yet we, whom you came to save and lead to that Bethlehem of eternal joy, stubbornly turn away from you. Forgive us, God and Lord of the Universe, and help us to walk alongside Mary and Joseph, thus giving us the courage to fight against, and triumph over, every adversity. Amen

'Divino', the Mexican American Cultural Centre, San Antonio, 1981

WEDNESDAY OF WEEK 4

JOSEPH: A COMPASSIONATE MAN

MATTHEW 1:18–21
Now the birth of Jesus the Messiah took place in this way. When his mother Mary had been engaged to Joseph, but before they lived together, she was found to be with child from the Holy Spirit. Her husband Joseph, being a righteous man and unwilling to expose her to public disgrace, planned to dismiss her quietly. But just when he

had resolved to do this, an angel of the Lord appeared to him in a dream and said, 'Joseph, son of David, do not be afraid to take Mary as your wife, for the child conceived in her is from the Holy Spirit. She will bear a son, and you are to name him Jesus, for he will save his people from their sins.'

Joseph finds out that Mary is pregnant and, because he's a compassionate person and not willing for her to go through public disgrace, he plans to separate from her as the law would demand. He certainly doesn't want to exact its full penalty, which would be stoning, but because betrothal was legally binding it would require a divorce, so he wants a secret divorce. In Judea, the right of cohabitation followed betrothal, but this may not have been the case in Galilee and the text makes clear that they had not lived together. Matthew, who is full of resonances from the Jewish scriptures, records that Joseph was spoken to in a dream, just as Joseph of the Old Testament was a dreamer. In his dream he is told that he can take Mary as his wife, that the child conceived in her is from the Holy Spirit, and that he must call him Jesus. He is to name the child because he is, in fact, the legal father. Despite the prophecy, Jesus is not called Emmanuel, though he is seen to be the fulfilment of this prophetic name, meaning, 'God is with us'. Jesus is a Greek version of the name Joshua or, in Hebrew, Jehosua, which has the probable meaning of 'Yahweh has saved'. There is a theme shared by both this Joseph and the Joseph of the Hebrew scriptures, namely that they are both involved in the saving acts of God. Through the first Joseph, God saved his family from famine, and now through this Joseph, God brings salvation in Jesus.

Joseph had an agonizing decision and his choice was to be compassionate. It was only after making that choice that God gave him encouragement and a new sense of direction. When he is described as a 'righteous person' in the passage, that means he sticks to the law, but in this instance he decided compassion was the better way of reflecting the law, and, perhaps because he was compassionate, he was ready to hear God's voice. In naming the child, he was claiming legal paternity, and so now he had the confidence to do this, even though he knew he was not the actual father. In those days,

Jewish law recognized that paternity was often difficult to determine and so the naming of the child publicly confirmed legal paternity. Many times we long to know God's will and we battle with decisions. We would certainly like to hear God's voice as clearly as Joseph did, but it is interesting to note that Joseph had to make his choice before he heard God's voice and he lived up to the best that he knew. Normally we make decisions by weighing up the evidence and the information that we have in front of us. We might also be inspired by compassion. It is only then, when we have made the decision, that we become more aware of God with us as we move forward.

PRAYER
Eternal Spirit, earth-maker, pain-bearer, life-giver,
source of all that is and that shall be,
father and mother of us all, loving God, in whom is heaven:

The hallowing of your name echo through the universe!
The way of your justice be followed by the peoples of the world!
Your heavenly will be done by all created beings!
Your commonwealth of peace and freedom sustain our hope
and come on earth.

With the bread we need for today, feed us.
In the hurts we absorb from one another, forgive us.
In times of temptation and test, strengthen us.
From trials too great to endure, spare us.
From the grip of all that is evil, free us.

For you reign in the glory of the power that is love,
Now and for ever. Amen
New Zealand Prayer Book

CHRISTMAS IN BETHLEHEM

Bishara Awad, Director of Bethlehem Bible College
Advent is preparing and, for me, it's preparing your heart for that big event on 25 December when Jesus was born. Because of that big historical event, the whole world has been changed, but particularly I want to see hearts to

be changed for God. Christmas for us, as a Bible College, is the happiest time of the year. It is a celebration for us—the choirs will be singing, and our own choir will be among them, by the Church of the Nativity there in the Manger Square. We invite people for a special celebration from the community. Last year we invited about 850 people and we fed them and we had a beautiful celebration. Everyone went out smiling and happy and so we are giving hope to the people, telling them you are loved by God, but not only by God, you are loved by his people. So these Palestinian Christians, they need the love of Christ and they have been more or less the underdog and they are the minority, and we are telling them, no, you are loved, stay here in the land and continue to live and be the light that Jesus wants you to be.

VOICES FROM BEIT SAHOUR ON HOPE

First voice: Abir Mousla

Abir Mousla is twenty-five years old and lives in Beit Sahour, right by the Shepherds' Fields. A Christian city on the West Bank, it became famous during the Intifada for the stand it took against paying taxes without representation. Abir teaches in Hebron in the Arab Evangelical School and is a Greek Melkite Christian. Greek Melkites—sometimes called Greek Catholics—are in communion with the Catholic Church and so celebrate Christmas on 25 December. Abir lives with her father and mother, and her brothers, in Beit Sahour. It is a relaxed atmosphere there, where boys and girls go about together, whereas in Hebron things are stricter.

In Bethlehem, in the schools we study with the boys and the girls in the same class. Here in Hebron it is different. Beit Sahour is now under the Palestinian Authority. We can't leave Bethlehem to go to Jerusalem and that's difficult... We live by the Shepherds' Fields but particularly feel the impact of what is happening on the hill Jabal Abu Ghoneim.

For the future, I hope for peace, to live a peaceful life, where I can go to any place I want without being restricted. I have friends in Jerusalem and Haifa and Jaffa and I can't see them. My Christian faith tells me to love others, to live with others and respect others. God teaches us to live with others in a peaceful way, and to help them and to love them.

At Christmas-time, we sing songs. Together with my friends, we learn many songs and sing them and after doing this on Christmas Eve, we go to Bethlehem, to the Church of the Nativity, to celebrate there at midnight.

Second voice: Dr Hadda Musleh

Abir Mousla put me in touch with her uncle, Dr Hadda Musleh, who is a lecturer and Professor of Psychology at Bethlehem University. He told me that Bethlehem University was started in 1973 by the Christian brothers. It's a university with a variety of faculties including arts, science, nursing, hotel management, physiotherapy, occupational therapy, education, and business administration. He said:

We have roughly 1900 students. Mostly they come from the middle part of Palestine, that is Bethlehem, Jerusalem, and the southern part, Hebron. We have few from the north. We have, of course, both male and female—the percentage of females is higher than males this year—and, of course, we have both Christians and Muslims. During the Intifada we experienced suffering like BirZeit University and our courses were interrupted. We were closed for almost three years by military order.

I was on the steering committee of the multi-lateral peace talks at the Orient House back in 1993/94. As a psychologist, I have to be hopeful, but as a person who was involved way back from the beginning in the peace process, when I look back four years and see where we are now, I don't see much hope...

Third voice: Ayman Abu-Zulouf

We have met Ayman Abu-Zulouf earlier in this book, on the Saturday of Week 2. He works with the Alternative Tourist Group in Beit Sahour. The Alternative Tourist Group organizes journeys around Palestine, introducing people to the local community and taking visitors to the ancient cities of Jerusalem, Jericho, Bethlehem, Nablus and Hebron. They link up especially with the people, both Christian and Muslim, and often organize for people to stay in local homes. They also organize work for volunteers and trips for students, which links with the University of BirZeit (near Ramallah) and also Bethlehem University. Ayman was a marvellous, friendly guide for us on our journey with the Amos Collective but we discovered that he had been in prison on several occasions, so we asked him how many times he had been in prison.

I have been six times in prison. They accused me of certain political things but there was no court, never a court, and I was jailed for two years altogether for no reason. My brother George was also imprisoned fourteen times and he spent four years in jail. My brother Rayad, he was arrested twice and he spent three years in jail, and my brother Tomi was arrested twice and spent one year in jail. George was tortured in prison when he was fourteen. It's been very hard for us, particularly over education, because of it being interrupted so much. It's very hard to feel we are the victims and we are persecuted, but it still doesn't give me the feeling to hate or to want revenge. I still have the hope that we can live here free, as good neighbours, because this is our only hope, this is the only thing for which I hope. I cannot hope for a war which would destroy both peoples.

THURSDAY OF WEEK 4

THE PEACEFUL COMMUNITY

Isaiah 11:1–6
A shoot shall come out from the stump of Jesse, and a branch shall grow out of his roots. The spirit of the Lord shall rest on him… His delight shall be in the fear of the Lord… With righteousness he shall judge the poor, and decide with equity for the meek of the earth… Righteousness shall be the belt around his waist, and faithfulness the belt around his loins. The wolf shall live with the lamb, the leopard shall lie down with the kid, the calf and the lion and the fatling together, and a little child shall lead them.

These hopeful words from Isaiah remind us of the character of the reign that will grow out of the 'stump of Jesse'. This peaceful kingdom will bring justice and equity and hope for the poor and the meek. They are words that are always before us, because there needs to be a constant coming of Jesus and the values of Jesus and the reign of God into places that are dark.

Archbishop Desmond Tutu, in an Advent message to the Church of the Province of South Africa, says:

It was precisely in the darkness where it looked like there was no way forward that the light which lightens everyone came into the world. And not into an ideal world: Christ came into a world that was at war, was rife with injustice, into a people under an army of occupation—think of how he was born and how quickly he became a refugee. This is the reality of so many of us. And in the incarnation God breaks into this and says, 'I am Immanuel, I am God-with-you. I am one who's not going to give you good advice from a safe distance. I enter the fiery furnace with you.' This is a message squeezed out of us so many times in the tragic situations we have been through. There is no other God who knows how to deal with chaos, through death and resurrection. How can we survive if we don't have this faith, and victory is ours through him who loved us? We have seen it!

The Advent message is for you as well. Give grace a chance! You have come into a culture of success. That's sad in many ways. It says the worst thing that can happen to a human being is to fail; that it doesn't matter what you succeed in so long as you succeed. If you can't pull yourself up by your boot strings you are out. Compassion, gentleness, become almost swear words. 'People must stand on their own feet'—yes, in a sense. But Christian faith says we are not made for independence but for interdependence. And maybe what will come from the weak and not-so-successful is a reminder to you that Christianity is a faith of grace. Grace is a gift. It says you are subsidized by God. One of my favourite Christmas hymns is O Little Town of Bethlehem with that wonderful verse: 'How silently, how silently the wondrous gift is given.' There was no fanfare—so very much like how the despised, the unimportant, come into this world. So God gives. Can you learn to receive, not just from us but from God?

Archbishop Tutu's words sum up the significance of light bursting into the darkness. 'God with us' comes in a humble way, in a silent and inconspicuous way, but it is reality and gives us hope in our struggles.

A STILL SMALL VOICE FOR PEACE

Menahem Benhayim is a former Israel Secretary of the International Messianic Jewish Alliance and former Secretary of the Messianic

Jewish Alliance of Israel. He wrote this open letter to believers during the mourning period for the late Prime Minister Yitzhak Rabin.

On that fateful Shabbat night I travelled from Jerusalem to attend the rally for peace and against violence organized in the Great Square in Tel Aviv. As an Israeli Messianic Jew living among his people, I felt obliged to identify with those who were protesting the violence and hatred spreading through our country during the past two years. I was distressed at the false messianism which was ready to risk civil war in order to push forward biblical prophecies.

Recently, I observed how Messianic Jews and Christians had entered the circles of hatred and slander in order to support zealots undermining the authority of the government, as if our Messiah was one of the ancient zealots who had more than once brought ruin and devastation to our land and people. As if our gospel were a gospel of blood and fire and not of reconciliation and peace, as if Yeshua had never said: 'Blessed are the meek for they shall possess the earth... Blessed are the peacemakers for they shall be called the children of God...

And then two pistol shots rang out that killed a wonderful man, as Leah Rabin put it in a broken voice to the crowds that had come to console her outside her home. I was reminded of the words of Yeshua concerning murder: 'You have heard that it was said, "You shall not murder" but I say to you that whoever is angry at his brother should be liable to judgment, and whoever says to his brother "raca" (good for nothing) shall be liable...'

What now? Shall Messianic Jews and Christian Zionists continue to uphold zealots? Thorny problems and difficult decisions remain for the people of Israel to cope with. Will they be hearing from believers of another way, a way of reconciliation, or will they play into the hands of extremists?

We are obliged to point to a different kind of messianic faith, the faith of Yeshua who sacrificed himself for us and for the world, and brought and still brings salvation relying on neither sword nor hatred. Brothers and sisters, this is a time to be renewed by the Spirit of our Redeemer, the Spirit of Immanuel, Prince of Peace!

Who is the man who desires life, to enjoy good for many days... seek peace and pursue it...

Menahem Benhayim, from *Seeking And Pursuing Peace*,
edited by Salim J. Munayer, published by Musalaha Ministry of Reconciliation

Menahem captures the Spirit of the Prince of Peace. We cannot turn the Bible into a book of oppression. We have another model and we can have a peaceful community if we follow that way.

PRAYER: THE WORK OF CHRISTMAS
When the song of the angels is stilled
And the star in the sky is gone
When the kings and princes are home
And the shepherds are back with their flocks
The work of Christmas begins:
To find the lost
To heal the broken
To feed the hungry
To release the prisoner
To rebuild the nations
To bring peace among the people
To make music in the heart

Howard Thurman, from the Christmas Card 'Christmas Begins',
Fellowship of Reconciliation USA

WHO WAS ST NICHOLAS (SANTA CLAUS)?

St Nicholas was born in Patara in the fourth century AD. He studied theology in the monastery in Xanthos. He became Bishop of Myra in Asia Minor and he died there. There are many stories that have sprung up round this bishop and his reputation seems to be that he was a caring person who dedicated his life for his people. He seems to have come from a rich family in Patara but he had a very generous spirit. He was committed to helping other people and it was his habit of giving gifts anonymously to the poor that particularly won him his reputation. He is reputed, as a bishop, to have treated everyone the same, to have been quietly spoken and good with advice. He was well known as a man of prayer and represented Myra in the Iznik council in AD325.

He became the patron saint of many different groups but particularly children, and tradition developed that he gave gifts to children on the eve of his feast day, 6 December. During the Reformation, many reformers not only wanted St Nicholas banished but also wanted Christmas itself to be dropped. However, the downplaying of Christmas had an alternative effect and St Nicholas became replaced with a more secular figure known as Christmas Man, Father Christmas or Papa Noel. It was the Dutch who were particularly reluctant to give up St Nicholas, and their name 'Sinterklass' is the root of Santa Claus, which was the English-speaking adaptation of the word, developed in the United States. Santa Claus had by now developed many of the aspects of Christmas Man—for instance, the workshop at the North Pole and the sleigh with reindeer. However, at the root of the story appears to be a generous-spirited man whose kind reputation won deep respect. He died on 6 December 343 and his body was put in the Orthodox church in Myra, which was then called St Nicholas.

HANUKKAH—AN END TO THE LONGEST NIGHT

These are some thoughts from Jewish theologian and peacemaker, Yehezkel Landau, on Hanukkah and power and powerlessness.

In the Talmud, which is the core of the rabbinical tradition in Judaism, a parable is told about Adam. From the time that Adam and Eve were created, the days were getting shorter from September through December. Adam started to get very worried that at this rate there wouldn't be any more light. Then, at the winter solstice, the process reversed itself and Adam realized that darkness was not going to prevail in God's creation. He therefore instituted the first festival of light precisely at the darkest time of the year. So the rabbis seem to be giving expression to the primordial origins of this celebration of light which preceded Judaism and all of our traditions—if you take this not as literally true but mythically and symbolically true. The rabbis are trying to give universal interpretation to this particular Feast of Lights which was the forerunner of Christmas.

The message of Hanukkah, to accentuate the divine light at the darkest time of the year, is supposed to be a reassuring, uplifting, inspiring counterpoint to the cycle of nature, but you can extend it to the headlines in the daily newspaper. On the surface, what seems to be true is whatever the politicians are doing on a particular story, but the real story isn't making it on to CNN. It's a much deeper one going back to the origins of the universe—it's programmed into the universe and we're supposed to be in tune with it. But we have become out of tune with the divine melody and with the divine rhythm programmed into the creation. That's what the whole sabbatical cycle is all about—including the jubilee—helping us to get back in tune.

Hanukkah is only referred to in a few lines in our canon because the books of the Maccabees are not included, like they are in the Catholic canon (the Apocrypha).

In the 63 volumes of the Babylonian Talmud, in a few lines on the tractate on Shabbat, the feast of Hanukkah is mentioned and the rabbis are asking, 'Why do we celebrate Hanukkah?' It's because of a special miracle that God caused when a cruse of pure olive oil, which had the seal of the high priest, was found in the defiled temple in Jerusalem when the Hasmonians—the Maccabees—liberated it from the Seleucid Greeks who had brought Hellenistic paganism to the holy of holies. This cruse of oil burnt for eight days instead of just one, while they were trying to bring more oil from further away. This miracle explains why we light the candles or olive oil for eight days in the Feast of Hanukkah.

It's not a celebration of the military or political victory. The rabbis did not want to emphasize this. They were writing after the destruction of the second temple. Not only had the Hasmonian dynasty corrupted itself, but the Romans had crushed two Jewish revolts. The rabbis did not want to reinforce the nationalistic and militaristic temptation to see redemption in political and military terms, but to recognize God working in more mysterious, less obvious ways. This message of the spiritual victory of God is reinforced in our liturgy on the Sabbath in the middle of the eighth day of the festival, when the portion read out in the synagogue is from the prophet Zechariah. This has as its main message the verse, 'Not by might and not by power, but by my spirit, says the Lord of hosts.' This has to do with the problems of power and powerlessness, and how the powerless can see redemption in their lives even though they are 'losers' in secular terms.

For most of our history, the last two thousand years, the Jewish people experienced the anguish of powerlessness. Now we're facing the anguish of power and how we use power responsibly, humanely. For me this is really the test of Jewish faithfulness, because the Torah presumed a sovereign commonwealth in which God's laws were written in people's hearts and were the standard by which the whole society lived. And yet every one of the Hebrew prophets (except Jonah, who was sent to the enemy capital of

Nineveh) addressed the sovereign rulers, the kings and queens, and the people, and reminded them that justice and loving kindness were the standards by which they were to be judged…

It's the integrity of the people, not the boundaries of the state, that determines the content of a state that calls itself Jewish. People who are territorially oriented, or think that Jewish rule over territory is above the golden rule, have mistaken the whole point of what our history has taught us and why we have survived all of these millennia without power.

FRIDAY OF WEEK 4
(Christmas Eve)

CHRISTMAS EVE CANDLES

LUKE 2:1–7

In those days a decree went out from Emperor Augustus that all the world should be registered. This was the first registration and was taken while Quirinius was governor of Syria. All went to their own towns to be registered. Joseph also went from the town of Nazareth in Galilee to Judea, to the city of David called Bethlehem, because he was descended from the house and family of David. He went to be registered with Mary, to whom he was engaged and who was expecting a child. While they were there, the time came for her to deliver her child. And she gave birth to her firstborn son and wrapped him in bands of cloth, and laid him in a manger, because there was no place for them in the inn.

Beloved in Christ, be it this Christmastide our care and delight to hear again the message of the angels, and in heart and mind to go even unto Bethlehem and see this thing which has come to pass, and the babe lying in a manger.

This is how the bidding prayer at the start of the service of nine lessons with carols for use at King's College, Cambridge, begins. It was written by Eric Milner-White and for many of us it has a familiar ring. Its beautiful words remind us that it is Christmas Eve and, in our imagination, we should go 'even unto Bethlehem'. After reminding us to mark the story in scripture of the loving purposes of God, it says:

But first let us pray for the needs of the whole world; for peace on earth and goodwill among all his people... and because this of all things would rejoice his heart, let us remember, in his name, the poor and helpless, the cold, the hungry, and the oppressed; the sick and them that mourn, the lonely and the unloved, the aged and the little children; all those who know not the Lord Jesus, or who love him not, or who by sin have grieved his heart of love.

Lastly, let us remember before God all those who rejoice with us, but upon another shore, and in a greater light, that multitude which no man can number, whose hope was in the word made flesh, and with whom in the Lord Jesus we are for ever one.

What a deeply moving prayer, which I love to hear on Christmas Eve, resonant with its tremendous sense of community and the values of the babe born at Bethlehem.

Back in the early 1980s, when I was touring in Poland, during the time of the Communist regime, I visited a place called Cieszyn on several occasions. Cieszyn is on the border of Poland and what was then Czechoslovakia, now the Czech Republic. In fact, the city had been divided and each country was cut off from the other, and although it was one town, you couldn't cross the bridge over the river and go to the other side. I sang in a beautiful little theatre in Cieszyn, which was like a mini version of the Vienna State Opera House. There was always a wonderful atmosphere for concerts there. But there was also a Christian bookshop in Cieszyn and the first time I visited it, I was deeply moved, more by what they *didn't* have than by what they had. There were just a few pieces of literature, which seemed to be more to look at than to take away or buy. They were, however, deeply proud of a new copy of Luke's Gospel that had just come in, in Polish, and they had plenty of copies of this. They gave me a gift from the shop, that they had made: it was a simple seven-branched candlestick. Since then we have always lit it on Christmas Eve, one candle at a time, praying for some troubled spot in the world, and we remember our friends in different parts of the world, in Poland or in Palestine. In those days we would always pray for our friends in the townships in South Africa, there would always be a prayer for Northern Ireland, and then for people we knew who had suffered through the year, or in memory of someone who had died. We still do it, as a family, and it's a poignant moment. It comes at the end of a family meal that we hold early in the evening on Christmas Eve. The meal is always raclette cheese, which is a twenty-year tradition for us, as a family, since a time when we celebrated Christmas Eve in Switzerland and sang *Silent Night* with the snow coming down in a beautiful mountainside setting. Now we have the meal, say the prayers, and then sing Christmas songs together.

To think about

Make sure there are some pauses in your schedule today for being quiet, for 'going to Bethlehem', for remembering the needs of friends and people around the world, for remembering the Christian community in Bethlehem tonight and in Beit Sahour and Beit Jala and Hebron, struggling to celebrate in difficult circumstances.

Prayer

Father, in this holy night your Son our Saviour was born in human form. Renew your Church as the body of Christ.

In this holy night Christians the world over are celebrating his birth. Open our hearts that he may be born in us today.

In this holy night there was no room for your Son in the inn. Protect with your love those who have no home and all who live in poverty.

In this holy night Mary in the pain of labour brought your Son to birth. Hold in your hand all who are in pain or distress today...

In this holy night shepherds in the field heard good tidings of joy. Give us grace to preach the gospel of Christ's redemption.

In this holy night the angels sang 'Peace to God's people on earth'. Strengthen those who work for peace and justice in all the world.

In this holy night strangers found the Holy Family, and saw the baby lying in the manger. Bless our homes and all whom we love.

In this holy night heaven is come down to earth, and earth is raised to heaven. Keep in safety all those who have gone through death in the hope of heaven.

In this holy night angels and shepherds worshipped at the manger throne. Receive the worship we offer in fellowship… with all the saints. Amen

From *The Promise of His Glory*, Church House Publishing,

© The Revd Michael Perham

SATURDAY OF WEEK 4
(Christmas Day)

THE GREATEST GIFT

LUKE 2:8–12, 16

In that region there were shepherds living in the fields, keeping watch over their flock by night. Then an angel of the Lord stood before them, and the glory of the Lord shone around them, and they were terrified. But the angel said to them, 'Do not be afraid; for see—I am bringing you good news of great joy for all the people: to you is born this day in the city of David a Saviour, who is the Messiah, the Lord. This will be a sign for you: you will find a child wrapped in bands of cloth and lying in a manger.' … So they went with haste and found Mary and Joseph, and the child lying in the manger.

So it's our first Christmas and the Western or Latin church celebrates the birth of Jesus—God with us—God, born as a human being, in a simple birth in Palestine.

THE TURNING AROUND OF ALL THINGS

We are talking about the birth of a child,
not the revolutionary act of a strong man,
not the breathtaking discovery of a sage,
not the pious act of a saint.
It really passes all understanding: the birth of a child
is to bring the great turning around of all things,
is to bring salvation and redemption to the whole human race.

What kings and statesmen, philosophers and artists,
founders of religions and moral teachers vainly strive for,
now comes about through a newborn child.

Dietrich Bonhoeffer, from *The Mystery of Holy Night*, Crossroad, 1996

Country singer Steve Earle wrote a song called *Nothing But A Child*. It's the story of the wise men setting out, bringing their gifts and travelling miles, following the star. And then he writes, 'But when it came to rest, they could scarce believe their eyes. They'd come so many miles, this miracle they prized was nothing but a child.' I've noticed that there's something slightly shocking about these words to many Christians. 'Why nothing but a child?' they ask. I, with them, when I first heard the words, wanted to say 'Yes, he was fully human but also divine,' yet somehow Steve Earle has captured it. For a moment we must stop and say 'nothing but a child', then his chorus goes:

Nothing but a child can wash those tears away,
will guide a weary world into the light of day.
Nothing but a child can help erase those miles
so once again we all can be children for a while.

© 1992 Duke of Earle/W.B. Music Corps and Warner Chappell Music Ltd

There's something very spiritual about those words, reminding us that we must become as a simple child to enter the kingdom of God. In the last verse of the song, he sees something special in the birth of every child: another chance of life, another hope. In this most simple of truths there is the deepest and most profound truth: that God asserted the value and worth of every human being when he entered the world as a vulnerable child.

God is with us in our humanity, in our frailty. We would like a God of power, we would like the suitable grandeur, and for the message not to be told first to despised shepherds. But God has his ways. The late Rabbi Hugo Gryn, when he was talking on *Desert Island Discs*, spoke about being in Auschwitz. He said that they had to ask themselves the question, 'Was God there?' And he said, 'Yes, God was present—but powerless.' Perhaps that gives us a clue to the meaning of the birth of Jesus in this style. He is 'God-with-us'. He is God with us in any situation, particularly in those most painful of times, but he's not an instant-answer God. He walks beside us in our vulnerable humanity and it's at this point that we discover the greatest hope of all. Vulnerable God of the manger moved on to become vulnerable God of the cross. But, though the candle flickers, it does not go out because he is also God of resurrection, and, as John Betjeman put it, God who was 'man in Palestine... lives today in bread and wine'. God is still discoverable in the tangible and in the ordinary, making these things sacred, making them miraculous. He is present in our neighbour and he is present with us.

LIGHTING THE CANDLE

Light the candle for this week, thinking of the hopes and fears of people of Bethlehem and the surrounding area, remembering those from the Shepherds' Fields. Take time to think of the hope and the light that Jesus brings into our world. Then pray the Christmas Prayer for those who are forgotten, and think of any people known to you for whom there seems to have been no room this year. Pray that they might find the reality of 'God-with-us'.

A CHRISTMAS PRAYER

Holy child of Bethlehem,
Whose parents found no room at the inn;
We pray for all who are homeless.

Holy child of Bethlehem,
Born in a stable;
We pray for all living in poverty.

Holy child of Bethlehem,
Rejected stranger:
We pray for all who are lost, alone,
All who cry for loved ones.

Holy child of Bethlehem,
Whom Herod sought to kill;
We pray for all who live with danger,
All who are persecuted.

Holy child of Bethlehem,
In you the eternal was pleased to dwell
Help us, we pray, to see the divine image
In people everywhere.

David Blanchflower, from *All Year Round*, British Council of Churches, 1987

No Room this Christmas—for the Villages of Al Nakba ('The Catastrophe')

For many Palestinians it is not only 'no room in the inn' but it is no room in their country. When the Zionist forces came in to Palestine in 1948, 418 villages were destroyed. There are also unrecognized villages like Ein Hod or Arab-El-Naim and Dumaida and El-Arain and Hawaled and Khamane. In 1948 the villagers of Ein Hod fled when they heard that the soldiers were coming to attack their village. They expected to be able to go back to their village after a few days, but when the war was over the new Israeli government introduced the law called the Absent Present law, saying that the Arab people existed but their villages did not. The new government wanted all the villages to be Jewish villages and so where there was a Palestinian village, they simply rubbed it off the map and said it didn't exist.

Ein Hod had become invisible. However, Ein Hod is like many other villages and the Association of 40 was formed. The aim of the Association of 40, which is a Christian Aid partner, is to get Ein Hod and the other unrecognized villages put back on the map. When this happens, the process begins to restore basic services such as roads, schools, water and proper health facilities, and this can take a long time.

However, when the Association of 40 was formed, it wasn't realized quite how many villages were awaiting recognition and facilities—nearly one hundred in total. Barbara Topp of Christian Aid asked Muhammed Abu El Haija of the Association of 40 what people in Britain could do to help the unrecognized villages. He said it would be a great help if people would write to the Israeli Prime Minister explaining the concerns of the Palestinian people whose villages are unrecognized. The more attention is focused on them, the greater are their chances of becoming recognized. It's also worth writing to the British Foreign Minister.

TO DO

There was no room for Jesus in the inn at the first Christmas. Let's make room for these invisible villages, for whom there has been no room in their own land for the last fifty years. A simple act this Christmas might be to write two letters on behalf of the unrecognized villages of Galilee and the Negev.

FIRST WEEK AFTER CHRISTMAS AND NEW YEAR

New Light, New Year, New Beginnings

During this week, as an aid to your prayers, have a candle which you light at a certain point each day with a chain around it to remind you of the huge debt crisis that is enslaving many parts of the world. When you light the candle, pray for the remission of debt and for justice. In 1997 the United Nations Development Programme estimated that 21 million children would die before 2000 unless the debt crisis is resolved. I hope that by now some significant steps will have been taken towards this, but pray that it will be carried through to fruition and that the voice of the world's poor will be heard as the twentieth century draws to an end and the new millennium begins.

TIME FOR JUBILEE

LEVITICUS 25:1–2, 4, 10, 12, 23, 39–41

The Lord spoke to Moses on Mount Sinai, saying: Speak to the people of Israel, and say to them: When you enter the land that I am giving you, the land shall observe a sabbath for the Lord… There shall be a sabbath of complete rest for the land… And you shall hallow the fiftieth year and you shall proclaim liberty throughout the land to all its inhabitants. It shall be a jubilee for you: you shall return, every one of you, to your property and every one of you to your family… For it is a jubilee; it shall be holy to you… The land shall not be sold in perpetuity, for the land is mine; with me you are but aliens and tenants… If any who are dependent on you become so impoverished that they sell themselves to you, you shall not make them serve as slaves… They shall serve with you until the year of the jubilee. Then they and their children with them shall be free from your authority; they shall go back to their own family and return to their ancestral property.

The year of jubilee is a fascinating concept. Land and animals were to rest, all property was to be restored to its original owner and all debts were to be cancelled. It's possible that it was never lived out but it is interesting that these instructions were part of the vision of the Hebrew scriptures. This chapter sees the sabbath first of all, not only as a rest but as a period of grace. A sabbath year is to be enjoyed every seven years, and then after seven times seven there is to be this year of release or year of jubilee.

It is important to note that this reparation was not merely making amends for personal sins committed, but was designed to repair the offences to God's holiness which had crept into the very fabric of the society over the 49 intervening years… The essential element of the jubilee year of release was therefore the enactment of forgiveness of debt. It reminded the Israelites that the land belonged not to them but to Yahweh their God… So whilst people could own, and were at liberty to sell the harvests from the land, the land itself was always to remain a gift of God to them, not to own, but merely to steward. They would remain always indebted to Yahweh but only for a limited period of years to one another.

Laurie Green, Bishop of Bradwell, from *Jesus and the Jubilee*, 1997

It is amazing how the commitment for the remission of Third World debt has caught people's imagination. It might sound quite a complicated issue, but in fact people are very much aware of the pain of debt. Whereas individuals or companies, when they are in debt, can be declared bankrupt, for a country this can't happen and the whole structure of society can be pulled down by the pressure of repaying interest rates.

I came across an example of this in Nicaragua. Through the Amos Trust, we support a school—The Avocado Tree School—up in a little town called La Concepcion, about twenty kilometres out of Managua. It is a very poor region with 85 per cent unemployment, so the local school run by the Baptist church is a beacon of hope to the community. People are desperate for their children to go there as they see education as a way for their children to break the cycle of poverty. The school was given grants by different international relief organizations in a deal with the government that they in turn would put in a considerable sum of money to help the school get off the ground. The government, however, has not paid anything as it has tried to be faithful to the Strategic Adjustment Programme of the International Monetary Fund, which is the route which is supposed to get them out of debt. Unfortunately, it means they have had to cut down on health and education and other practical things within the society like the building of roads, and the result is that poverty is much more obvious on the streets and in a place like La Concepcion.

The problem for the school is that they need to charge $2.50 in school fees a month. This is not a big figure to people in Britain— maybe it amounts to £1.70. We could buy a cup of coffee and a newspaper for that and not think twice about it, but about 85 per cent of the parents are unable to meet this figure for their children to go to school, even though it is the thing they most desperately want. Similar stories come from country after country around the world and the debts were often imposed on societies in ways that can only be described as immoral. For example, in Zaire, it was well known that President Mobutu and his government were corrupt. An investigation was done by the IMF and the report said that there was complete corruption and so no more money should be lent. The following year, more money was loaned than ever before. Of course, none of this money got through to the ordinary people, yet it's they who now must carry the burden of it since President Mobutu has gone.

The concept of jubilee is that people should not become slaves for ever more, whether literally or in debt. So society takes a pause and the earth has a pause and people have a fresh start. What better time than at the beginning of a millennium to say, 'Let's start again.'

When Jesus, in Luke 4, quotes from Isaiah 61 in the synagogue at Nazareth, it is thought that he was inaugurating a permanent jubilee year, when he echoed the words 'to proclaim the year of the Lord's favour'. Jesus was suggesting that these are the ongoing values by which we should live, the new values of God's reign. Jesus was very inclusive, however. He said that this was not simply a jubilee for the Jewish community, but was to be liberation for all nations. This was too much for his listeners, who took him out and tried to throw him off the brow of the hill, but Jesus was proclaiming justice and jubilee for all.

PRAYER

O God, to whom we owe more than we can count, in our desire to control all that will come to be we hold your other children in the grip of debt which they cannot repay, and make them suffer now the poverty we dread. Do not hold us to our debts, but unchain our fear, that we may release others into an open future of unbounded hope. Through Jesus Christ our Saviour. Amen

Janet Morley

We cannot resign from the world as it is… Each of us individually has the responsibility to use his or her own judgment as to how we can make the maximum contribution to building a better world for humankind to live and work in.

Julius Nyerere, the former President of Tanzania

RESTORED TO WHOLENESS

MARK 2:1, 3–12

When he returned to Capernaum after some days, it was reported that he was at home... Then some people came, bringing to him a paralysed man, carried by four of them. And when they could not bring him to Jesus because of the crowd, they removed the roof above him; and... they let down the mat on which the paralytic lay. When Jesus saw their faith, he said to the paralytic, 'Son, your sins are forgiven.' Now some of the scribes were sitting there, questioning in their hearts, 'Why does this fellow speak in this way? It is blasphemy! Who can forgive sins but God alone?' At once Jesus perceived in his spirit that they were discussing these questions among themselves; and he said to them, 'Why do you raise such questions in your hearts? Which is easier, to say to the paralytic, "Your sins are forgiven," or to say, "Stand up and take your mat and walk"? But so that you may know that the Son of Man has authority on earth to forgive sins'—he said to the paralytic—'I say to you, stand up, take your mat and go to your home.' And he stood up, and immediately took the mat and went out before all of them; so that they were all amazed and glorified God, saying, 'We have never seen anything like this!'

Ched Myers, in his book *Say To This Mountain* (Orbis, 1996), points out that in this incident Jesus is challenging the debt system. He has just challenged the purity system when he healed a man with skin disease (Mark 1:40–42), and now he does the same thing with the debt system. Myers points out that 'debt and sin were virtually interchangeable terms', and that the debt code was under the jurisdiction of the scribes. When Jesus debates over scripture, he is involved in social criticism about the authority of priests or scribes. When Jesus is faced with the paralysed man, as Laurie Green says, he 'responds by going straight to what it is which binds the paralysed man to the bed. It is the burden of sin, the heaviness of his debt to God, which immobilizes him. But as Jesus pronounces the man's sins forgiven, some scribes... accuse Jesus of usurping the authority which only God can have, since the debt of sin which caused the illness is owed to God alone. Jesus proves his authority by asking the man now to walk, and in doing so usurps not God's prerogative but the authority which the priests have taken upon themselves to pronounce what was clean, and which sin or debt was to remain unforgiven.' So the debt is forgiven and Jesus is shown to have brought about a significant transformation and Jesus asks the paralysed man to show that this full release has occurred by picking up his bed and walking.

Jesus has restored the man to wholeness, to the community, and to self reliance, and so has wrested from the scribal and priestly class their authority on earth to release from debt and sin and has declared it to be the free gift of Yahweh.

Laurie Green, *Jesus and the Jubilee*, 1997

So this too is an example of Jesus living out the jubilee in his ministry. A political struggle now occurs between Jesus—the Son of Man or the human one—and the class system of the scribes and priests who claim that they have authority on earth. Jesus is perceived to be the one who critiques the structures that perpetuate oppression and this is seen to be a function of the Son of Man.

As we head towards a new year, what are the systems that need to be critiqued? The politics of domination that leave people exploited and oppressed. These things can happen at many levels within politics, that is, the ordering of society, but also within the church and the ordering of religion. Are people being dominated or manipulated? Walter Wink says of Jesus' ministry:

Looking back over Jesus' ministry, what emerges with bracing clarity is the comprehensive nature of his vision. He was not intent on putting a new patch on an old garment, or new wine in old skins... he was not a reformer, bringing alternative, better readings of the law. Nor was he a revolutionary, attempting to replace one oppressive power with another... he went beyond revolution. His assault was against the basic presuppositions and structure of oppression itself. Violent revolution fails because it is not revolutionary enough. It changes the rulers but not the rules, the ends but not the means.

Walter Wink, *The Powers that Be*, Doubleday, 1998

When you light your candle today, pray to be made whole. Pray for situations where chains of domination or oppression need to be broken, both in big international ways, like Third World debt, but also in small ways, in our own community. Take time to think about issues, both large and small, that our churches should be facing in carrying on the work of Jesus, of bringing wholeness in community.

A CHRISTMAS MESSAGE OF HOPE FROM SABEEL LIBERATION THEOLOGY CENTRE

The coming of Christ into the world holds many meanings for many different people. For us as a Palestinian Christian Community, it is primarily a message of hope. Although we do feel despair when we look around us, we are nevertheless filled with hope when we look to Christ and reflect on his coming.

Indeed it is hope that is our greatest source of empowerment and so, despite all the difficulties of this past year, we join our voices with the apostle Paul and affirm that 'we are saved by hope' (Romans 8:24).

Luke's narrative of the birth of Christ and the angels' proclamation to the shepherds is familiar to us all. There are key phrases in the message of the angels that are especially full of hope and liberation for those of us living under occupation, as were the shepherds two thousand years ago.

'Do not be afraid: for see—I am bringing you good news of great joy: to you is born this day a Saviour.'

For people who live in situations of oppression this is great news. Fear is to be dispelled, joy will replace it. A Saviour, a liberator, is coming who will usher in peace.

This great Christmas news, however, is sent to us in a most peculiar way, in that our Saviour and liberator arrived in the form of a child born in a stable (Luke 2:12). To many it may seem absurd that God challenged the strong and mighty through such a vulnerable creature. This baby was not born into the powerful political or religious establishment of that day, but rather into the poor and marginalized section of society. God chose to become incarnate in a child—his parents could only find shelter in a cave and, as an adult, he had no place to lay his head (Luke 9:58). Salvation, it appears, derives from the most unlikely people and places. This is the paradox of a God whose very essence is bound with the refugees, the outcasts, the abused and the oppressed. So it is that Paul could very well write, 'For God's foolishness is wiser than human wisdom, and God's weakness is stronger than human strength' (1 Corinthians 1:25).

This year's Christmas message to those in power is that they cannot ultimately disregard and discount God. To those who appear 'powerless' the message lies in deriving hope from a baby, the most vulnerable of all beings, and from a cave, the most improbable place of power. So it is that we must continue to rely upon God's seeming illogic and our collective action to bring about a lasting peace.

Adapted extract from *Cornerstone*
published by Sabeel Liberation Theology Centre

Every effort to strengthen the marginalized
Every struggle to empower the dispossessed
Every challenge to might as right
Is the celebration of our freedom
Let us invest in such a jubilee.

Christmas message from Paul Divakar, a Christian Aid partner
from Darc Shittoor, India

PRAYER
Compassionate God, as we walk on the journey with you towards wholeness, we are inspired by the example of Jesus, where he confronted the systems that hold people back from dignity and from liberty. Thank you for the news of salvation from the most unlikely of places—a stable and a cave. Thank you for your strange ways that bring us hope, and for your foolishness that confounds the wise. Amen

RABBI JEREMY AND HIS CAR MECHANIC

I had a conversation with my car mechanic recently. I think he noticed my car sticker that says, 'Israel for peace' and we started talking about the political situation. The mechanic confessed that he was on the right wing, but he had some Palestinian friends, although not many. I said, 'For me my Palestinian contacts and friends are a major part of my life and it's really very special to me that I make these friendships.'

He then spoke about there being no future in partnership or communication and I said, 'But I feel that there's wonderful possibilities of mutual enrichment and appreciation in living together. I'm optimistic, because I think there can be a happy end here. On the other hand, I'm very depressed about the recurring electrical problems in my car.' So he says to me, 'Well that's the difference between us. I can solve small problems but the bigger problem I'm depressed about, but you get tripped up by the small things but have an outlook which is positive about the ultimate things.'

I was very happy to have that moment of truth with him and it was a pleasant conversation despite our differences. I really would love him to meet, and to get to know, my Palestinian friends. They are a lifeline for me. I don't think I could live here without that, and without the acceptance I've had among Palestinians.

Rabbi Jeremy Milgrom

TUESDAY OF WEEK 5

THE MASSACRE OF THE INNOCENTS

Matthew 2:16–23

When Herod saw that he had been tricked by the wise men, he was infuriated, and he sent and killed all the children in and around Bethlehem who were two years old or under, according to the time that he had learned from the wise men. Then was fulfilled what had been spoken through the prophet Jeremiah: 'A voice was heard in Ramah, wailing and loud lamentation, Rachel weeping for her children; she refused to be consoled, because they are no more.' When Herod died, an angel of the Lord suddenly appeared in a dream to Joseph in Egypt and said, 'Get up, take the child and his mother, and go to the land of Israel, for those who were seeking the child's life are dead.' Then Joseph got up, took the child and his mother, and went... to the district of Galilee. There he made his home in a town called Nazareth, so that what had been spoken through the prophets might be fulfilled, 'He will be called a Nazorean.'*

Over the first two chapters of his Gospel, Matthew introduces Jesus to the readers in various ways. In the genealogy he is seen as the son of Abraham and the Son of God, at the end of chapter 1 he's seen as Emmanuel and early in chapter 2 he's seen as the son of David. Now, in this passage, he's seen as the new Moses, maybe the new Jeremiah, and also as a Nazorean—perhaps the new Samson. Matthew never misses an opportunity to remind people of the strong links with the Hebrew scripture, though his suggestion that 'he will be called a Nazorean' is a fulfilment of prophecy is a puzzle, as there is no direct text with which this corresponds.

Herod was known as particularly cruel and, although this story of the massacre of the innocents is not corroborated in other histories of the period, Herod's brutality is well recognized. Herod will cling to power at any cost, and he even sees a baby as a threat to his power. This incident reminds us of Pharoah's command to kill all the male children of the Israelites prior to the exodus, and Matthew uses the moving words from Jeremiah about Rachel weeping for her children and refusing to be comforted. Children are often in the forefront of suffering in conflict situations or in poverty or hunger. Many of these situations are caused by the desire for power to the detriment of everyone else, and millions of street kids in the cities of our world are left utterly vulnerable.

My son, Tom, was working with one street kid in East London, South Africa, called Siseiko Sisulu. The workers would spend time with the children and gradually introduce them to the shelter where they hoped they would be able to come and stay. Siseiko was one in that situation. He was fourteen years old but very small for his age. In the middle of the night, Tom was called out by other street kids to say that Siseiko had been raped and beaten up. When Tom got there, Siseiko was still alive and was rushed to hospital, but tragically he died soon afterwards. Tom, and the other street kids, determined that Siseiko would be remembered, that his life was not for nothing, and huge numbers of them attended his funeral. They also tried to bring pressure to bear in the local community to make sure that his death would be properly investigated. Maybe today the Holy Innocents are the street kids of this world, who should be the future and yet who are simply the victims of a world that has such a huge imbalance between rich and poor.

As we read on in the chapter, we discover that Joseph has another dream—still reminiscent of the Old Testament Joseph. In the end, the little family heads up to Nazareth, probably because Joseph, being involved in the building trade, could get work not far from Nazareth at Sepphoris, where Herod Antipas was rebuilding his capital.

To do

Today, light the candle particularly for children, whether they are suffering in war or through hunger or through poverty and arriving on the streets. Pray for their protection and for people working to help them.

Prayer

God, please stop injustice,
The killing of innocent children
By violence at home and in faraway lands.

God, please stop injustice,
The killing of innocent children
By poverty at home and abroad.

God, please stop injustice,
The killing of innocent child's spirits
By vanity and greed in our land and others.

God, please stop injustice,
The assault on precious child dreams
By neglect and apathy near and far.

God, please stop injustice,
So our children may live
And love and laugh and play again.

From *Guide My Feet* by Marian Wright Edelman, Beacon Press

Painful Honesty from Jerusalem (Al-Quds)

This is an interview with Mahdi Abdul-Hahdi, the Head of PASSIA, the Palestinian Academic Society for the Study of International Affairs.

PASSIA is the think-tank for Palestinian academics, to encourage research studies. They publish studies on Palestinian issues and keep people updated with the latest information about Palestine and Palestinian history. They train young Palestinian graduates in international affairs. They also organize conferences. These are (1) Palestinian-to-Palestinian dialogues, concerning relationship building within their own community; (2) briefings for diplomats and congressmen, senators and members of parliament, and other visiting delegations; (3) meetings with Israelis, politicians, academics, and other professionals; and (4) inter-faith dialogues with Muslims, Christians and Jews.

Dr Mahdi Abdul-Hahdi told me a little about his own family history first:

The Abdul-Hahdis go back to the seventh century in Palestine. They came with Islam, with prophet Mohammed, in the seventh century, and during the 1800s they governed Acco and Nablus in Palestine. My grandfather was a governor of Beirut, and my uncle was the major activist in the Palestinian national movement during the British mandate. My father is a judge. All our family are judges or lawyers—this is the family profession.

Dr Mahdi Abdul-Hahdi is a Muslim, but he says that as a believer in God, he tries to be receptive, frank and sincere in meeting with other people from different religions without judging them in advance; meeting them as human beings and trying to understand them. He says:

Here in Palestine, we are in the centre of the holiness of all messages, of all beliefs, of all the good and the bad of life. You are here in Jerusalem where any Muslim or any Jew or any Christian would feel that this is his capital. This is his centre, the closest spot God looked at or dealt through, and all prophets had something to do with this place—you can put on the place a label, and this label is holiness. Some people would like to be exclusive in their relationship with this holiness, 'this is theirs', but we differ with them on this. This should not be exclusive to one people at the expense of the other people, and this should not be exclusive to one faith at the expense of the others. This should be open to all faiths. But if we are wise enough and if we are good believers, we will not be exclusive, we will listen and we will allow the voice of reason to prevail.

I asked Dr Mahdi if he was hopeful, and he was quite painfully honest.

No, I'm not hopeful. So many people are really depressed, angry and frustrated, with no hope… If Islam, Judaism and Christianity confront one another we are doomed to failure. But if we can bring people together to share, to dialogue and to understand each other, we might get somewhere… The language of the gun, the language of the bullet, is a sad story of pain and suffering… We want to maintain the stretching out of our hands to yesterday's enemy, who we believe could become a friend and neighbour.

WEDNESDAY OF WEEK 5

NEW WAYS

Matthew 25:31–32, 34–36, 40

When the Son of Man comes in his glory… all the nations will be gathered before him, and he will separate people one from another… Then the king will say to those on his right hand, 'Come, you that are blessed by my Father, inherit the kingdom… for I was hungry and you gave me food, I was thirsty and you gave me something to drink, I was a stranger and you welcomed me, I was naked and you gave me clothing, I was sick and you took care of me, I was in prison and you visited me… Truly I tell you, just as you did it to one of the least of these who are members of my family, you did it to me.'

These extraordinary words of Jesus are unique to Matthew's Gospel. In this memorable passage Jesus reminds us that our actions are important, indeed we shall be judged by them. Did we care for the weaker members of society? Sometimes Christians have tried to suggest that the phrase 'the least of these who are members of my family' refers only to the faith community, but when you look further down in the passage, you see that this is not the case, for it refers to the human family. There's no way out!

As we approach such an important new year, what kind of resolutions will we make? It may be a good time to review our lifestyle. Can we do without certain things in order to help others? Those of us who live in Western society often grumble because we do not have enough and yet, in real world terms, we are extremely wealthy. We could simplify our lifestyle, we could release more resources.

Our world is deeply divided and this should challenge us. The combined wealth of the world's seven richest men could wipe out poverty and provide basic social services for the quarter of the world who live in severe need. The cost of completely eradicating poverty is one per cent of global income. Effective relief to the twenty worst affected countries in the world is the equivalent of building Euro Disney, or less than the cost of one Stealth bomber. Nearly one third of the developing world's population live on less than a dollar a day. More than 800 million people do not have enough to eat.

Now read on in Matthew 25. '"Lord, when was it that we saw you hungry or thirsty or a stranger or naked or sick or in prison and did not take care of you?" And he will answer them, "Truly I tell you, just as you did not do it to one of the least of these, you did not do it to me"' (vv. 44–45). The deep imbalance in our world is because we do not follow the jubilee principles of Jesus. Our churches should be at the prophetic forefront of the movement to bring change, to bring healing and hope within community. Yet, sadly, they often drag behind. Let these words act as a real spur to us as we enter the millennium.

PRAYER
Lord, help us to spend less time on what we need to have, and more time on who we need to be and what we need to do as your hands and feet and voice of mercy and justice in the world. Amen

BE THE HANDS OF JESUS
Be the hands of Jesus
Be the feet of Jesus
Let the heart of Jesus be our guide

I was hungry and you gave me food
I was thirsty you gave me drink
I was a stranger and you welcomed me
I was naked and you clothed me
I was sick or in prison and you came

Be the hands of Jesus
Be the feet of Jesus
Let the heart of Jesus be our guide

TO DO

Light a candle for those who, like Mahdi Abdul-Hahdi and others, work to bring people together. Especially light it for those for whom the candle of hope is now burning low, and say this Greek Melkite petition:

We pray that God will heal the pain of those who suffered the loss of family or of land; that bitter hurt may be transformed into healing and love.

For all those, Jew and Arab, who have the courage to meet together in the quest for understanding, reconciliation and peace.

For Palestinian Christians who, more easily than most, can reproduce a pattern of life close to that of Jesus, and yet who find that today, it is his experience of rejection and homelessness, and of living in a land ruled by others, that is the hardest to bear.

For all Jews in Israel, that sensitivity and goodwill may prevail in the affairs of their country, and for those in the diaspora.

For Muslims and Druze, with their belief in one God, and devotion to the land of their forebears.

For all peoples, that thy light may shine upon them, that the spirit of justice and mutual forbearance may be established among them. To thee we cry, O Lord, hear and have mercy.

Melkite petition

A POPULAR ARABIC CAROL:
ON THE EVE OF CHRISTMAS

On the Eve of Christmas   Hatred will vanish
On the Eve of Christmas   The earth will flourish
On the Eve of Christmas   War will be gone
On the Eve of Christmas   Love will be born.

When we offer a glass of water to a thirsty person
  it is Christmas
When we clothe a naked person with a gown of love
  it is Christmas
When we wipe the tears from weeping eyes
  it is Christmas
When the spirit of revenge dies in me
  it is Christmas
When in my heart I no longer want to stay apart
  it is Christmas
When I am buried in the being of God
  it is Christmas

Cornerstone Christmas 1997, published by Sabeel Liberation Theology Centre

Thursday of Week 5

NEW CREATION

ISAIAH 65:17–24

For I am about to create new heavens and a new earth; the former things shall not be remembered or come to mind. But be glad and rejoice for ever in what I am creating; for I am about to create Jerusalem as a joy, and its people as a delight. I will rejoice in Jerusalem, and delight in my people; no more shall the sound of weeping be heard in it, or the cry of distress. No more shall there be in it an infant that lives but a few days, or an old person who does not live out a lifetime; for one who dies at a hundred years will be considered a youth, and one who falls short of a hundred will be considered accursed. They shall build houses and inhabit them; they shall plant vineyards and eat their fruit. They shall not build and another inhabit; they shall not plant and another eat… They shall not labour in vain, or bear children for calamity… Before they call I will answer, while they are yet speaking I will hear.

This is a vision of a wonderful new world that God is creating, where justice is so strong that the sound of weeping will no longer be heard.

Children won't die, people will build houses and live in them themselves, they will eat the fruit of the trees they plant. This is the other side of the picture as it currently exists in the Bethlehem area. I think of the people sitting beside their demolished homes, people whose land has been used to build new settlements or roads to service new settlements. I think of Abuna Elias Chacour, who has taken me to the ruins of his village Ba'ram, which is one of the 418 Palestinian villages destroyed in 1948. As he talks about the trees, and shows them to me, I realize how much people love the land and love the trees that they planted, yet from which another now eats.

What these verses assert is a world where there is space for everyone, where no one grabs at the expense of another, where even Jerusalem becomes a focus for joy and delight. I remember, soon after the peace talks began, being in Palestine/Israel on a beautiful weekend and travelling from Jerusalem to Bethlehem and on to Nazareth. Everyone was full of optimism; they caught a glimpse of what could be. I thought, how wonderful, we will soon forget about all the conflicts of the past, communities will exist side by side dependent on one another. 'The former things shall not be remembered.' It seemed as if it was a possibility, but it was soon to be destroyed in a welter of bombs and violence. But this passage reminds us that the vision can become a reality and we need to pray and work towards it.

The reference to planting their own vineyards and eating their fruit brings to mind the story of Naboth's vineyard in 1 Kings 21. It's a story which has come to mean a lot to many Palestinian Christians who have a problem with the Exodus story as a paradigm for liberation. The reason for this is that when the Israelites came out of Egypt and were liberated, they then came into the land of the Canaanites, the Hittites, the Amorites, the Perizzites, the Hivites and the Jebusites. This was the land they were given, indeed this was the land flowing with milk and honey. The problem was that, although they had had liberation, they then had to deprive others of their liberty in order to possess the land. For this reason, Palestinian theologians have prompted us to look beyond this model, and people like Canon Naim Ateek have particularly focused on the story of Naboth's vineyard in 1 Kings 21, as he finds this more relevant to his people's concerns, because it demonstrates God's unwavering commitment to justice.

You may remember the story. Naboth owned land that he had inherited from his ancestors not far from Beisan (Beth Shean). His property adjoined the palace of King Ahab. The king wanted to expand his estate and to buy Naboth's land, but Naboth refused because to him his land was sacred, as is very common in Middle East cultures. The king was angry and his wife, Queen Jezebel, decided to plot against Naboth. Naboth was taken to court, accused of blasphemy, and he and his sons were stoned to death. Elijah then confronted Ahab, saying that he and Jezebel would be punished for this behaviour. This encourages Naim Ateek because it shows God's commitment to justice. The land belonged to Naboth and his family, and he was powerless and defenceless and then victimized, but God saw what was going on and sent his prophet to reflect his viewpoint. Naim Ateek says:

Yahweh's ethical law, championed by the prophets, operated impartially: every person's rights, property, and very life were under divine protection. Whenever injustice occurred, God intervened to defend the poor, the weak, and the defenceless.

Both Ahab and Jezebel died brutal deaths and Naim Ateek says:

I fully recognize that today, as in Naboth's time, many people still relish the exercise of strict justice—'an eye for an eye and a tooth for a tooth'... I am repelled by such a formula, which only creates more injustice. I would plead for justice with mercy.'

Maybe this is the clue to the kind of society that we see prophesied about in Isaiah, the society where justice and mercy go hand in hand, where it's not allowed for some to dominate while others are powerless, but where the wolf and the lamb shall feed together.

Mitri Raheb is from an ancient Bethlehem family, who have lived there for hundreds of years. He is pastor of the Evangelical Lutheran Christmas Church in Bethlehem and in his book *I Am A Palestinian Christian* (Fortress Press, 1995) he also addresses this story of Naboth's vineyard.

His concern arose because of a situation with a local man, called Daher, and his family who have a beautiful vineyard on a lovely hilltop. Because of the political situation, the family found it impossible to obtain the water necessary to cultivate their land. Whenever Daher's family looked across from their land to the neighbouring settlement, only five hundred metres away—a settlement with a biblical name, Daniel's Oasis—they could see that people had everything they needed in the way of water, so that their vineyard bloomed whilst Daher's vineyard wilted. The settlements wanted to confiscate his vineyard because of its position on the hilltop and so the Daher family came to see Mitri with the Israeli military order to confiscate it. Mitri was not totally surprised. What was clear to him was that the biblical tradition set by King Ahab and his wife Jezebel was being followed.

The office of prophet throughout the Old Testament is that of intervening wherever a responsible authority breaks down. Persons and institutions who are in this prophetic tradition cannot keep silent. Neither can the Church, which honours the prophetic inheritance... Therefore the Church could not fail to act with regard to the expropriation of Daher's vineyard. We were forced to attempt to prevent it. We therefore started a drive with the participation of Christians of various denominations, Muslims and Jews from the peace movement.

At the time he wrote his book, he said:

The matter is still unresolved. Will the Daher family be able to keep the vineyard of its forefathers or will it be confiscated and turned into a settlement? Will the whisperings of Jezebel succeed, or will the words of the prophets be heard?

PRAYER

Wonderful Counsellor, give your wisdom to the rulers of the nations. Mighty God, make the whole world know that the government is on your shoulders. Everlasting Father, establish your reign of justice and righteousness for ever. Prince of peace, bring in the endless kingdom of your peace. Almighty Lord, hear our prayer, and fulfil your purposes in us, as you accomplished your will in our Lord Jesus Christ. Amen

From *The Promise Of His Glory*, Church House Publishing

As you light your candle today, and see the chain around it, focus on this vision and pray that it will become a reality—that the chains will be broken and justice will take root and flourish.

INDEPENDENCE DAY

Rabbi Jeremy's Palestinian friends have been helping him to do some adjustments to his flat. He says:

One of them was very friendly with my dog and that's unusual for Palestinian society, not used to having dogs as house pets. I asked him whether he had a dog at home and he said, 'No.' I asked, 'Do you want to have a dog?' He said, 'I'd love to, but I only live in forty square metres and I've got five kids, so there's no room for a dog.' So I asked him, 'If you had the money and could build, where would you build a bigger house?' He said, 'I would build in my village.' He knew, and I knew, that he meant the abandoned village of 1948. It wasn't about moving into Bethlehem or moving out of the suburbs of the refugee camp, where people who have made it economically live. We then started talking about visits they used to make to the old village—or what's left of it—and these were great moments as we chatted in the months of construction.

Some of the families came from one village and some came from another. I know about one of the villages. I had an interesting experience last year on Independence Day, which occurs in April or May, twenty days after Passover. I took a bike ride with a friend and we thought we would be as far as we could be from the usual tumult and celebration of Independence Day. I didn't want to be part of this jingoistic celebration, so we went down to the foothills of Jerusalem on our bikes. Suddenly, we came upon a sign that said, 'No photography, military zone'. I recognized that this was the back yard, or the back fence, of one of Israel's atomic arsenals. My heart sank. This was not how I wanted to spend this holiday. I turned around and looked back to the east. There I saw my Palestinian friend Omar's village. I recognized it. Here I was, right in between what they call in America 'a rock and a hard place'. I was in between the nuclear installation and the Bedouin village, which has the scar of the unforgivable lapse in our own sensitivity. It was a rude awakening on a picnic, to recognize that I had not escaped the bigger implications of this political event, but I was actually in physical contact with it.

LOVE ONE ANOTHER

1 JOHN 4:7–8, 19–20

Beloved, let us love one another, because love is from God; everyone who loves is born of God and knows God. Whoever does not love does not know God, for God is love… We love because he first loved us. Those who say, 'I love God,' and hate their brothers or sisters, are liars; for those who do not love a brother or sister, whom they have seen, cannot love God whom they have not seen.

Here we are on the verge of a new year, of a new century, and of a new millennium. What an exciting time! And yet as we look back over this millennium, it has been a time of brutality and cruelty, often in the name of religion, beginning with the Crusades and ending with holocausts. This century has been a century when more people have died as martyrs for the Christian faith than ever before. The niches at Westminster Abbey have been filled with statues of ten modern martyrs. Maximillian Kolbe, who died in Auschwitz-Birkenau. After him there is Martin Luther King, the great black leader and advocate of non-violence, who was shot dead in Memphis. Archbishop Oscar Romero of El Salvador, who identified with the poor and, in the end, died for them. And so the list goes on. Christians from all around the world, who followed the way of love and paid the ultimate price. They made choices; choices that all their lives had prepared them for. As we develop our characters, by choosing the way of love and by choosing the way of Jesus, we have to keep making choices day by day. In the end, when we come to a time of suffering or struggle, we will know what is the right decision to take.

Hopefully, for most of us the path will never lead to martyrdom, but it may be costly in other ways. But we will try to do what we know is right. This passage reminds us how to live, what should underpin our resolutions and our lifestyle as we enter a new year. Love of our neighbours is the key. When we love our brothers and sisters, people know that we also love God. Perfect love casts out fear. One of the figures in one of the niches at Westminster Abbey is Archbishop

Janani Luwum of Uganda, who was killed by Idi Amin. When all the church leaders were summoned by Idi Amin to Kampala and ordered to leave the room, Archbishop Janani said, 'They're going to kill me. I'm not afraid.' The way of love was stronger than fear and, in the end, stronger than death. What choices will you make in the new year? What issues are on your mind at the moment? Think them through in the light of these words of self-sacrifice in today's passage.

For some, there may be the question of vocation. This is often a difficult one, and one that has to be approached practically as well as with inspiration. I've never found better words than those of Frederick Buechner, who says this:

*There are all different kinds of voices calling you to do all different kinds of work, and the problem is to find out which is the voice of God, rather than that of society, say, or the super ego, or self-interest. By and large, a good rule for finding this out is the following: The kind of work God usually calls you to do is the kind of work (a) that you need most to do and (b) that the world needs most to have done. If you really get a kick out of your work, you've presumably met requirement (a) but if your work is writing deodorant commercials, the chances are you've missed requirement (b). On the other hand, if your work is being a doctor in a leper colony, you've probably met requirement (b) but if most of the time you're bored and depressed by your work, the chances are that you've not only bypassed (a) but probably aren't helping your patients much either. Neither the hair shirt nor the soft berth will do. **The place God calls you to is the place where your deep gladness and the world's deep hunger meet.**

From Wishful Thinking—A Theological ABC, Harper & Row, 1973

God has given us gifts and personalities, and where the deep satisfaction and the world's deep need meet is where we'll find a way forward. And what will drive us? Love, that this passage talks about, rather than the self-interest which is so often the dominant issue within our society.

PRAYER
Eternal God, as we come to the end of another year, we thank you that throughout it all you walked beside us. We ask you to forgive us the wrong

*that is past and to put it behind us and to walk forward with your love
and hope in our hearts, and may we abide in your love this year and love
others because you first loved us. Amen*

CHRISTMAS IN NAZARETH

Najwa Farah

The changes of the seasons were always exciting, like a ritual in our
lives as a family and as a community. When winter came, it gave us
such joy to come back from school to a cosy home. In the evening,
my mother would boil carrots and roast chestnuts on the brazier while
we sat on floor mattresses and cushions or on low wicker chairs. We
would also have plates of dried figs, raisins and walnuts... As a child
I did not like autumn, a melancholy season, but then I began to look
forward to Christmas. In Nazareth, Christmas was more low-key than
Easter, which was and still is called the Great Feast. There were
Christmas trees in public buildings and in some (mainly Protestant)
churches and church schools. Catholic churches put more emphasis
on the crib and the stable-cave.

I should mention that the Western communities in Nazareth
followed the well-known Julian calendar, while the Eastern churches
followed their own calendar, so that Western Christmas was on 25
December, while the Orthodox Christmas was on 6 January.
Sometimes there might be a whole forty days between the Orthodox
and Western Easters.

Epiphany fell on 6 January, the Greek Orthodox Christmas. Special
sweets were prepared with very thin pastry, some of it filled with nuts,
cinnamon and sugar, and some fried and dipped in syrup. On 15
January, it was my brother 'Irfan's birthday. All our extended family
would come for a big tea, and my father engaged the best sweet-maker
to come to the house and prepare two huge trays of *kenafeh* (shredded
rolls of wheat with syrup, cheese or walnuts). My mother played the
organ and we all sang hymns, followed by games. After my brother's
birthday, my mother would take down the Christmas tree and the
Christmas decorations were put away for another year, *inshallah* (God
willing).

From *A Continent Called Palestine* by Najwa Farah (SPCK), 1996

WAITING FOR OUR SOULS TO CATCH UP

Mark 1:35–39

In the morning, while it was still very dark, he got up and went out to a deserted place, and there he prayed. And Simon and his companions hunted for him. When they found him, they said to him, 'Everyone is searching for you.' He answered, 'Let us go on to the neighbouring towns... And he went throughout Galilee, proclaiming the message in their synagogues and casting out demons.

It's a New Year, and no doubt we have all stayed up very late to see the New Year in, so before we rush to make any resolutions or new plans, let's pause. One Christmas some friends of mine from the Scottish team of Christian Aid sent this message:

On a Himalayan expedition, after several days non-stop walking, the Sherpas simply sat down and would not go on. For a whole day, they sat, and eventually the explanation came—they had been going too fast, they said, their souls had not been able to keep up with them; now they were waiting for their souls to catch up with them again.

I think I have been there. I think I recognize this condition—the need to take a pause, to breathe, to be quiet, to let the soul catch up. Sometimes I've done it by sitting quietly in a church, sometimes by walking in the countryside, sometimes by just sitting at home. A friend of mine, the poet Stewart Henderson, was asked, when he was performing at a Christian event, to write a biography beforehand which included what he liked to do at home. Amongst other things, he put down 'to sit and do nothing'. This wasn't considered good enough as it was not sufficiently active so it was left out, but he pointed out to me that he did like to do this, to simply sit. I think those were the moments when his soul caught up with him.

Prayer seems to be an important part of all this—not the hyperactive prayer when we talk and talk and talk, but those times when we sit quietly and bring certain things into the presence of God without talking too much. Perhaps simply by taking time to breathe and focusing our mind on one simple thought or one simple prayer. Thomas Merton said:

There is a pervasive form of temporary violence to which the idealist fighting for peace by non-violent methods most easily succumbs: activism and overwork. The rush and pressure of modern life are a form, perhaps the most common form, of its innate violence. To allow oneself to be carried away by a multitude of conflicting concerns, to surrender to too many projects, to want to help everyone in everything is to succumb to violence. More than that, it is co-operation in violence. The frenzy of the activist neutralizes one's work for peace. It destroys one's inner capacity for peace. it destroys the fruitfulness of one's work, because it kills the root of inner wisdom which makes work fruitful.
Quoted in *Peacemaking Day By Day*, Pax Christi

If we are to do the tasks of proclaiming and living the gospel message, the casting out of the demons of domination and oppression, then those moments when the soul catches up, when we draw strength from God, are of vital importance.

I have come to treasure prayer more these days. Often I use a simple form of daily prayer which I find in the New Zealand Prayer Book, and later in the day I cherish those rare moments—the quiet and the pauses, the breathing space that I sometimes find, where I can stop for a while and draw strength. Those are valuable moments, and, I must be honest, when I look again at Thomas Merton's words, I am aware that I have surrendered to too many projects. So I do make a New Year's resolution that there will be more of these pauses. When we're too busy, the soul has to move awfully fast!

PRAYER
Father, my days are numbered, and you have counted them all, and know how long I have to redeem time.
So, help me to avoid evaporating my spirit through busyness, and

make me able to stand and stare, guiltlessly; for then I may offer you my
wonder at your world, and might discover my life in a wider perspective.
Amen

Lighting the Candle

This week there has been daily lighting of the candle, thinking particularly of people who are suffering because of the situation of Third World debt. Pray for jubilee in this area, and pray for the others we have met this week who are struggling against the odds and need to see jubilee made visible.

Prayer for a new Millennium

O God who gave us life,
and in whose arms we die,
you know us as we are,
understand what we have been,
and see what we shall become.
We give you back our lives
that you may make them new:
generous, committed to hope,
and fearless to do your will;
that your whole creation
may live to praise your name
now and for ever.
Amen

Janet Morley/Christian Aid, *Gift of Life*

EPIPHANY — CHRISTMAS 2

An Eye-Opener

Jesus, as we travel far and fast,
Lead our minds back to the wise men following your star,
And forward to the day
When all will see your shining light.

Jesus, light of the world,
Let your bright star stand over the place
Where the poor have to live;
Lead our sages to wisdom and our rulers to reverence.

O God, by the leading of a star
You revealed your Son Jesus Christ to the Gentiles;
Grant that your whole church may be a light to the nations,
So that the whole world may come to see
The splendour of your glory;
Through Jesus Christ our Lord. Amen

From The New Zealand Prayer Book

REST FOR YOUR SOULS

MATTHEW 11:28–30

'Come to me, all you that are weary and are carrying heavy burdens, and I will give you rest. Take my yoke upon you, and learn from me; for I am gentle and humble in heart, and you will find rest for your souls. For my yoke is easy, and my burden is light.'

ISAIAH 40:28–31

Have you not known? Have you not heard? The Lord is the everlasting God, the Creator of the ends of the earth. He does not faint or grow weary; his understanding is unsearchable. He gives power to the faint, and strengthens the powerless. Even youths will faint and be weary, and the young will fall exhausted; but those who wait for the Lord shall renew their strength, they shall mount up with wings like eagles, they shall run and not be weary, they shall walk and not faint.

These wonderful words of Jesus from Matthew's Gospel remind us again to find rest for our souls, and this time it is in Jesus. Jesus says, 'Take my yoke upon you' as opposed to the yoke of the Torah or the yoke of the kingdom of which the rabbis spoke. Jesus says that his yoke is easy because his teaching is a lot shorter and focused on essential things. Once again it's Jesus the liberator, not bringing a huge complex system, but rather—because he's humble and gentle and he himself is the way—he liberates us and walks beside us. I've linked this with the passage in Isaiah, which also talks about how 'those who wait for the Lord shall renew their strength… they shall not be weary'. This is the God who restores our strength.

As I was preparing this book, and journeying around the Bethlehem area, I became aware that many people that I met are exhausted with the struggle. Life under the peace process has become worse for them, and the Christian community and peacemakers of this part of the world are weary. Yet, as it says in Galatians 6:9, 'Let us not grow weary in doing what is right, for we will reap at harvest-time, if we do not give up.'

Rima Nasir Tarazi wrote a prayer for the Sabeel conference in February 1998 in Bethlehem. It was based on a song she had written earlier, from an album called *The Dreams Of My People—Palestinian songs written in Occupied Palestine*. She had given a dedication: 'To our brethren who write our country's history with their blood, to our sons who teach us how to transform our wounds into song and how to draw a smile from the wells of despair, to our children who create the new dawn with their patience and strength, I dedicate these songs.' The prayer is like a dialogue between the pain of one person and the response of the God who says, 'Come to me all you that are weary.'

A. O God, hear my prayer, for I live in misery and darkness. In your name, O God, they tortured me and dispersed my people, in your name they ravished and prevailed. O God, hear my prayer.

B. What they claim in my name is false.
I am the light of righteousness, love and life.
I have spent my blood for you. I have offered my life to save you.
How would they oppress and transgress in my name?
I am the light of righteousness, love and life.

A. They usurped our country, they partitioned it and robbed it.
They ploughed our fields and planted them with our bodies.
They uprooted our villages and replaced them with their homes.

B. Come to me, all you that are weary and are carrying heavy burdens, and I will give you rest.

A. They attacked us in our abodes and threaten us with destruction.
They pushed us into dispersion and squeezed us into tents.
They burned us with bombs and drowned us with blood.
They enchained us and threw us in prison cells.

B. Come to me, all you that are weary and are carrying heavy burdens, and I will give you rest.
I bring to you good tidings. Prisoners will be released,
Sight will be restored to the blind.
Your rights will be restored

And your land will be restored.
I have spent my blood for your sake.
I have offered my life to save you.
I am the light of righteousness, justice and life.

A. O God, hear my prayer.

Rima Tarazi's prayer helps us to deal with the character of God. God is not the oppressive figure that has sometimes been claimed, but rather the one who, in the suffering servant or in Jesus, says, 'I am gentle and humble in heart. Come to me, you that are weary, and I will give you rest.' Rima links words from Isaiah 61 and Luke 4 about the good news. It is God who brings in the values of jubilee, the values of justice and freedom from oppression. This is the God of hope.

The same God who says, 'Come to me, all you that are weary' is the one who says, 'They that wait upon the Lord shall renew their strength.' He is the one who has given us the principle of taking a day off each week. Joan Chittister wrote a remarkable article for *The Tablet* on 22 March 1997 called 'The Lost Sabbath'. In it she said:

Scholars of the Talmud tell us that the reason the Sabbath was created was not because God needed rest but in order to sanctify rest, to demand rest of us so that by regularly resting in God we could ourselves become new people. In our stress-filled, over-busy world, we need to restore this concept of Sabbath. We have lost the Sabbath spirit and take no notice as a culture of the starvation of soul and the exhaustion of mind that result from depriving ourselves of reflection. We have turned Sundays into weekdays and wonder what has happened to neighbours and nature and our nervous systems.

Sabbath days should be when we allow ourselves time out to look at life in fresh and penetrating ways, when we are called to worship what deserves to be worshipped and to dismiss from the centre of our souls what does not. But our society has found other things to worship on the Sabbath. We worship consumerism by turning Sundays into some of the biggest shopping days of the year.

Joan Chittister

DO NOT JUDGE

JOHN 8:3–11

The scribes and the Pharisees brought a woman who had been caught in adultery; and making her stand before all of them, they said to him, 'Teacher, this woman was caught in the very act of committing adultery. Now in the law Moses commanded us to stone such women, Now what do you say?' They said this to test him, so that they might have some charge to bring against him. Jesus bent down and wrote with his finger on the ground. When they kept on questioning him, he straightened up and said to them, 'Let anyone among you who is without sin be the first to throw a stone at her.' And once again he bent down and wrote on the ground. When they heard it, they went away, one by one, beginning with the elders; and Jesus was left alone with the woman standing before him. Jesus straightened up and said to her, 'Woman, where are they? Has no one condemned you?' She said, 'No one, sir.' And Jesus said, 'Neither do I condemn you. Go your way, and from now on do not sin again.'

This beautiful passage is a late addition to John's Gospel and indeed some versions of the Bible print the verses at the end of the Gospel. Others even include it in Luke, after Luke 21:38. It was not added to the manuscript until the third century, but it is a passage which reflects the spirit of Jesus in a very special way.

It is interesting to compare this passage with a story in the Apocrypha, in Daniel and Susanna. This is sometimes printed as a separate book, and sometimes printed at the end of Daniel. It is the story of a beautiful and devout woman called Susanna who is married to Joakim. She is very religious and has been brought up according to the law of Moses. Two elders of the community spot her when she is walking in her garden, and it says, 'They were obsessed with lust for her.' In the end they both creep separately into the garden because they want to seduce her, and bump into each other and agree on a plot. So when she is alone in the garden, they come in and say to her, unless you 'consent and yield to us' we shall give evidence against you that there was a young man with you. Susanna groans and says, 'I see no way out. If I do this thing, the penalty is death; if I do not, you will have me at your mercy. My choice is made: I will not do it. It is better to be at your mercy than to sin against the Lord' (vv. 22–23, NEB).

So the elders then bring her in front of the people and the judges, and witness against her. They immediately sentence her to death and she cries out to God in despair, pointing out that she's guiltless, and it says, 'The Lord heard her cry.' As she is being led off to execution, Daniel stands up and says, 'I will not have this woman's blood on my head.' He realizes she has spoken the truth and he insists that the trial must be re-opened. He interviews the men separately and finds out that their stories do not tie together. The two men are then dealt with by the law of Moses for giving false evidence, and are put to death.

Jesus would no doubt have been familiar with this story and so it makes a very interesting comparison. The two elders say, 'We saw them in the act', which is reminiscent of what the accusers of the woman caught in adultery said in front of Jesus, 'This woman was caught in the very act.' In both situations the appeal was made to the law of Moses and a woman's word was not respected in a court of law at that time—a woman could not be a witness. Consequently, it was very easy for women to be found guilty and to suffer the death penalty.

Jesus, then, says, 'Let anyone among you who is without sin be the first to throw a stone at her.' Then we find that the people drift away, one by one. Jesus questions the motives of those who are the accusers and this is an echo of his words, 'Do not judge so that you may not be judged.' In the story of Susanna it is startling to see how the two elders who witness against her are immediately accepted in their viewpoint. Again, in the incident of the woman caught in adultery, it is male elders who bring the woman to Jesus—and there is no sign of her male partner.

The elders want to test Jesus to see if he will obey the law of Moses and have her stoned. In fact, Jesus takes it one step further. Whereas Daniel proves who is guilty and who is innocent and has the guilty party stoned, Jesus allows people to think about their own situations and then to slip away. We should not judge, because we are all guilty in some way or other; therefore let us support one another rather than condemn, and then go and sin no more.

There is another interesting difference in the two stories, in so far as Susanna is clearly innocent of the accusation, whereas in the woman's encounter with Jesus, that may not be the case. Jesus points out that she is not condemned, so can go on her way, and says, 'From now on do not sin again.' Maybe all of us need to be reminded of a fresh start like this. We do not stand condemned in front of God, but rather we can go on our way with hope, with a fresh start, and lead a better life. An encounter like this with Jesus lifts us up and reminds us of our dignity, and that the journey goes on. We walk away with a spring in our step and hope in our heart.

PRAYER
O God, guard us against hypocrisy—against pointing the finger at others when we should be dealing with our own motives and the things we have done wrong. Teach us to be generous in our spirits and forgiving in our attitudes, as we are forgiven. In your name. Amen

TUESDAY OF WEEK 6

THE TWO STEPHENS

ACTS 7:54–58
When they heard these things, they became enraged and ground their teeth at Stephen. But filled with the Holy Spirit, he gazed into heaven and saw the glory of God and Jesus standing at the right hand of God. 'Look,' he said, 'I see the heavens opened and the Son of Man standing at the right hand of God!' But they covered their ears, and with a loud shout all rushed together against him. Then they dragged him out of the city and began to stone him; and the witnesses laid their coats at the feet of a young man named Saul.

26 December is the day on which Stephen, the first Christian martyr, is remembered. Stephen, who was chosen as a deacon to serve the early Church, was described as a man 'full of faith and the Holy

Spirit'. In Acts 7 he gives a very long speech that traces God's activity from Abraham through Joseph and Moses to David and Solomon. He finishes by being critical of the people for killing the prophets and they react with great anger and stone him to death for blasphemy.

Last year I took part in a service on the street in Well Hall Road in Eltham, South East London, to commemorate the death of another Stephen on 22 April 1993—Stephen Lawrence. This Stephen was the victim of a racial attack. He was not the first. Rohit Duggal, a young Asian teenager, had been stabbed to death in 1992, also in a racial attack in the same road. The failure to find anyone guilty of the attack on Stephen and, indeed, the extraordinarily slow process even of arresting anyone after the attack, despite the local community having given information to the police, have caused a long and difficult pilgrimage for Doreen and Neville Lawrence. This has culminated in an enquiry to find out what happened and why the police failed in their investigations. There is a plaque in the pavement where Stephen was killed. The plaque had been desecrated, but at the time of the memorial service it had been restored. However, it was damaged again soon afterwards.

On the night of Stephen's death, Louise and Connor Taaffe were walking down the road after a prayer meeting at the local Catholic church when they saw him collapse. Connor says this:

The black teenager's name was Stephen—the name of the first Christian martyr. When I first saw him running... I sensed immediately that something had happened and thought to myself that he might have been involved in a fight, that he might have been partly to blame for provoking some aggression. I later learned that Stephen had done nothing at all to provoke the attack, other than bearing a black skin. He was innocent, as Stephen's namesake was innocent.

While I was crouching down beside him, I saw a wide flow of thickened blood. The image of that red blood on the grey concrete paving stones has stayed with me, and the thought that keeps coming back to my mind... is that Jesus freely chose to spill his blood for us... Stephen was accompanied by the prayers of fellow Christians in his dying moments—not only from Louise and myself but, incredibly, from an off-duty policeman and his wife who were returning home from another prayer meeting. In those last moments, Louise whispered into Stephen's ear, 'You are loved.' Louise and I went back to the prayer meeting... I explained... what had happened and the whole prayer meeting brought the situation before God... There in front of the blessed sacrament, it was as if Stephen's death was joined through prayer to that of Christ. I had a strong sense of how much Stephen was loved, as Louise has said. Perhaps because Stephen had 'the gift of a black skin'— in the words of the black Bishop of Croydon at one of the many services at the site of the murder—we were being reminded how much God loves people, all people, all races, all colours... I was told that, on a television programme one Sunday morning, Stephen's father... spoke of his son's death as a 'sacrifice'. The death of God's son was fruitful. The death of the first martyr Stephen was fruitful too, for 'the blood of the martyrs is the seed of the church'. Mr and Mrs Lawrence, I believe the death of your son, your Stephen, will also bear fruit even if only in ways that we cannot yet see.

The Tablet

The tremendous struggle of Doreen and Neville to try to get justice has brought home to many people in our society how deep the racism is and how much we need to set our house in order. There has been a string of people killed in racist attacks in our land and Stephen's death and also Stephen's enquiry have brought home to people the sheer horror of racism. The arrogance of the five young men who appeared at the enquiry accused of the murder will be an abiding memory in people's minds and a recognition that evil can go very deep within society and within individuals. The evil of racism must be exorcised in all of us, in our churches, in our communities, and on our streets. The words Louise repeated to Stephen as he lay dying were, 'You are loved, you are loved' and no more valuable words could have been spoken. They are words we need to say to one another; to show how much each human being is respected and valued by a loving God, and that we too should treasure one another.

YOU ARE LOVED STEPHEN LAWRENCE
Rolan Adams, Rohit Duggal, Orville Blair, Stephen Lawrence
How long must the list go on
Who can stop the disease that eats at the heart of England
How many more will have gone

Louise and Connor Taaffe left the church where they'd prayed
Found Stephen on the street so there they knelt and stayed
Louise whispered in his ear—trying to find words of hope
'You are loved, you are loved' were the words that she spoke

You are loved—Stephen Lawrence
You are loved—she whispered in his ear
You are loved—Stephen Lawrence
She bent down and she whispered in his ear.

Garth Hewitt, from the album *Stronger than the Storm*,
© Chain of Love Music

PRAYER
*Servant God, there have been too many martyrs—too much blood has
been shed. Teach us to remember that when the blood of Jesus was shed
that was enough. You are the father and mother of all humanity. You give
us the strength to root out any racism that exists in ourselves and to walk
the road of the gospel that says the barriers are down. Amen*

WEDNESDAY OF WEEK 6

GIVING THANKS IN JENIN

LUKE 17:11–16
*On the way to Jerusalem Jesus was going through the region between
Samaria and Galilee. As he entered a village, ten lepers approached
him. Keeping their distance, they called out, saying, 'Jesus, Master,
have mercy on us!' When he saw them, he said to them, 'Go and show
yourselves to the priests.' And as they went, they were made clean.
Then one of them, when he saw that he was healed, turned back,
praising God with a loud voice. He prostrated himself at Jesus' feet
and thanked him. And he was a Samaritan.*

Somewhere on the road between Samaria and Galilee, Jesus goes into
a village which tradition puts as the village of Jenin or En-Gannim.
   In *Guide to the Holy Land* Eugene Hoad says of Jenin:

It is… surrounded by gardens of carob, fig and palm trees, irrigated by a tiny brook which flows, whenever it thinks fit, right through the town. There is a small Latin parish.

Jenin is clearly the ancient En-Gannim of the Bible and was part of the tribe of Issachir… It is the same village mentioned by Josephus under the name of Ginaea, as situated on the frontier line between Samaria and Galilee at the entrance of the great plain where the Samaritans assaulted a caravan of Galileans on their way to Jerusalem and killed a great number of them.

So maybe somewhere in the region of Jenin, in the northern part of the West Bank, is where this incident occurred.

Jesus initially tells the lepers to do what the law of Moses requires, namely, 'Go and show yourselves to the priests.' It is only when they have turned to do this that they discover that they have been made clean—and one, who turns out to be a Samaritan, turns back, praises God, and comes to Jesus and thanks him. So here was a group of people separated from normal society by their disease, including a Samaritan, who was racially separated from the Jewish community, so twice an outcast, who comes back with his heart overwhelmed with gratitude. Luke is making it clear that Jesus is the one who restores people to human wholeness and to relationships with one another. It seems that Luke is also pointing out that the Samaritan is the one who really sees and understands what has happened, and that in his understanding he finds salvation and wholeness. The Jews and the Samaritans did not mix, and yet here we find that one of the party of ten lepers is a Samaritan. In their common suffering, racial and national barriers get broken down. So, too, in the new reign of God that Jesus is inaugurating.

There is an echo here of 2 Kings 5 where Naaman, an army commander from Syria who has leprosy, is sent down to meet the king of Israel. The king is shocked that he is expected to provide healing for Naaman, but when Elisha hears of this he tells the commander to come and meet with him, and instructs him to wash in the Jordan. The fact that Naaman is a foreigner is key in this story. He is appalled at the request that he should go and wash in the little river of Jordan, but, when persuaded to do so by his servant, is immediately healed. Like the Samaritan in the story of the ten lepers, he too returns to give thanks, and, in the same way, also recognizes God's involvement in his healing.

Why didn't the others return? Were they so excited that they had been healed that they rushed to get the official clearance from the priest? Who knows? But Luke wants to make it clear that this double outcast is made a whole member of the community through Jesus. Giving thanks is a healing activity of itself. It is good, in the morning, to thank God for each new day, and the opportunities that are ahead, for life and for breath, for family and for friends. It is also good, in the evening, to thank God for the things that have happened in the day, and for the beautiful things we have seen, as well as to ask forgiveness for the things we have done wrong. It is good to thank one another, so that people recognize they are appreciated. All this keeps relationships and community whole.

PRAYER

O God, here we are at the beginning of a new year. May we take time to look back with gratitude to the way that you have led us, and the fact that you walk beside us on our journey. We thank you for the good gifts that you have given us, for the beauty that surrounds us, and for family and friends. May we always be people of grateful hearts. And we thank you for our creation, preservation, and all the blessings of this life, but above all for your immeasurable love that we find in Jesus Christ. Amen

MY BETHLEHEM IDENTITY

Pastor Mitri Raheb, whom we met on page 132, is a Christian Palestinian whose roots go back in Bethlehem for hundreds of years. He says:

I was born in Bethlehem on 26 June 1962, into a family that took root in this city a very long time ago. The Raheb family has lived in and around Bethlehem for many centuries... My identity was stamped by the fact that I was born in this particular place. I feel I have something like a special relationship to David and to Christ—a relationship developed not only by way of the Bible, not only through faith, but also by way of the land. I share my city and my land with David and with Jesus. My self-understanding as a Christian Palestinian has a territorial dimension. I feel that I am living in a continuity of locale with these biblical figures, sharing the same landscape, culture, and environment with them... That is why this city of Bethlehem and this land of Palestine are enormously important to me. They do not merely help me to live, they are a part of my identity... Although Palestine was once a Christian land, with the passage of time more and more Christians were assimilated [into Islam], and their number decreased. The Christian Palestinians of today are nothing else than the Christian remnant that has remained steadfast despite all the persecutions in Palestine. These Christians live where the most important events of revelation took place. About 30,000 live in and around Bethlehem, the city of the incarnation; about 20,000 live in and around Jerusalem, the city of the cross and resurrection; and approximately 100,000 Christian Palestinians live in and around Nazareth, the city of the annunciation. About 320,000 other Christian Palestinians live in the Diaspora...

The Holy Sites

In times of war, both Christians and Muslims sought refuge in the great and historically significant churches. I can still remember the Six Day War in 1967: shortly after war broke out and Israel started shelling Bethlehem, my mother carried me to the Church of the Nativity, where we and many other Christian families from Bethlehem found refuge.

At the same time, Christians have always felt responsible for protecting and defending these churches and sites... The fact that Christian Palestinians have refused to abandon these holy sites, despite massive pressure, demonstrates that the holy sites are almost meaningless to them if there is not a Christian community living and worshipping there. The stones of the church need the living stones, but we living stones need a space and a locality in which to live and to celebrate.

The Witness of Arab Christians

By the fourth century at the latest, Bethlehem was inhabited exclusively by Christians... More than 130 monastic communities were established in the wilderness in the immediate vicinity of Bethlehem between the fourth and the sixth centuries. The wilderness began to bloom, not with flowers but with monasteries. These monasteries played a considerable role in Christian piety, Palestinian theology, and Middle Eastern church politics of the following centuries...

Arab Christians are an inseparable part of the world of Islam. Dialogue with Muslims is a necessary and important aspect of Arab Christians' life and survival... There are about 14 million Christians in a world of more than 200 million Muslims. This, too, is typical of the history of Arab Christians. They have hardly ever been the people with power, which is what prevented them from being persecutors and exploiters. But this also meant that they were never quite spared suffering... Arab Christians were sometimes made forcibly aware that their Western co-religionists cultivated a Christianity strange to them. Arab Christian existence was strongly linked to the sign of the cross from the very beginning. To them, the cross was the reality of a suffering church rather than the inheritance of a triumphant church. Western churches, on the other hand, related the sign of the cross to power, vested interests, and expansion. To some extent, the slogan became 'crusade' rather than 'follow in the way of the cross'.

THURSDAY OF WEEK 6

EPIPHANY AND THE SECOND CHRISTMAS EVE

MATTHEW 2:1–5

After Jesus was born in Bethlehem of Judea, wise men from the East came to Jerusalem, asking, 'Where is the child who has been born king of the Jews? For we observed his star at its rising, and have come to pay him homage.' When King Herod heard this, he was frightened, and all Jerusalem with him; and calling together all the chief priests and scribes of the people, he inquired of them where the Messiah was to be born. They told him, 'In Bethlehem of Judea; for so it has been written by the prophet.'

6 January is the day of the celebration of the Epiphany and also Christmas Eve for the Orthodox Church. In the old Eastern tradition, several things were celebrated at one time, not only the birth of Jesus but also his baptism in the Jordan and his 'manifestation' or revelation of who he was by his miracle at the wedding of Cana. In the Western

church, we connect Epiphany with the 'manifestation' or showing of Jesus to the Gentiles, i.e. the wise men.

On two occasions I have had the opportunity to celebrate this second Christmas Eve at the Church of the Nativity in Bethlehem. I wrote of the first occasion in *Pilgrims and Peacemakers* and it was a difficult time because the local Christians could not join us from the village of Beit Sahour as they were under curfew. However, the second time I was there was just after Bethlehem had been handed back to the Palestinian Authority. I was there with my wife Gill and a large group of friends from around the world who had come to celebrate the consecration of Riah abu-El Assal as the Anglican Bishop in Jerusalem. The service took place on 6 January 1996, and in the evening we all went to Bethlehem to join in with the Orthodox Christmas Eve celebrations.

Such was the excitement in Manger Square that at first we could not get in and the new Palestinian Authority police struggled to hold people back. On the previous occasion, local Christians were unable to be there, but now they were free to celebrate the birth of the Prince of Peace. There was the sense that it was a new country emerging— the land of Palestine was at last reappearing. Eventually we got in and worked our way towards the front where we were to see an extraordinary sight. The previous Anglican Bishop of Jerusalem, Bishop Samir Kafity, and the newly appointed Bishop, Bishop Riah, were leading President Yasser Arafat around, up the steps from the Grotto and then around to the different congregations who were worshipping in the Church of the Nativity that night. It was a glorious and chaotic moment, something like a liturgical rugger scrum! But perhaps it symbolized something of the feeling of that weekend: that hope was rising again in this forgotten community.

We were only to hear vaguely about an event in Gaza that happened that weekend that was to change the whole history of the peace process, when the Israeli security forces put a bomb in the mobile phone of a man known as 'the engineer'—and killed him. This act was to lead to bomb blasts in Jerusalem as retribution for the killing, and the downhill spiral that was to include such events as the terrible massacre of the Palestinian refugees in the UN post at Qana in Lebanon. And so this awful downhill spiral has gone on.

For me, the simplicity of the Church of the Nativity seems to give it a special atmosphere, and I love to go there and light a candle and pray. I have always found the eastern side to have more of an atmosphere than the west, which is called St Catherine's. However, at the end of the Sabeel conference in February 1998 there was a very moving service in St Catherine's when, with people from all around the world, we lit candles and sang and prayed for justice and peace to come to Palestine. I wrote this meditation during that service, as we shared bread together.

HOUSE OF BREAD

The light of God has come into this world
To the House of Bread—given for the world
It started in Bethlehem—broken for all
Bethlehem—House of Bread

Womb of our hope, let all people be fed
As we share bread in the House of Bread
From our neighbours in the mosque next door—
                                        I hear the call to prayer
As a candle of hope is lit in the House of Bread

Eating bread together means... eternal bonds
                                of love and friendship
In Bethlehem, where God visited our world
We still hear God through echoes of the angel's songs
And our high calling is still to give glory to God
                                and still to be peacemakers

In the House of Bread the Spirit of the living God rejuvenates us
To work in love
for peace with justice...
And never to despair

In the House of Bread the Spirit of the living God
Has refreshed us to commit ourselves to each other
In joy and pain
To work for healing and reconciliation

In the House of Bread broken for all
The Spirit of the living God has renewed us
God has become our liberator—our Sabeel—
our way and our living water

The light of God has come into this world
To the House of Bread—given for the world
It started in Bethlehem—broken for all
Bethlehem—House of Bread

Garth Hewitt, St Catherine's Church, Bethlehem, February 1998

THE HOLY LAND IS THE FIFTH GOSPEL

Zoughbi Zoughbi

My message to Christians is that it's good to visit the holy stones, but
it is much more wonderful to meet with the living stones and to be
acquainted with the rolling stones—the socio-political situation. I
feel, as St Jerome said, the Holy Land is the fifth Gospel, and I would
say that the people here could also be interpreted as the fifth Gospel.
So it is time to meet the Palestinians here who have witnessed for
Christ for the last two thousand years. You should really come and see
those people who are still living in the land and relate to the land and
are here in Bethlehem and Jerusalem. You could see Jesus Christ
through this place. It means a lot for us, so don't come here and miss
the opportunity to meet with the living stones.

I feel we need to wake up the Christian West in general, to tell
them there are at least 15 million Arab Christians in the Middle East
who are your brothers and sisters, who don't need anything from you,
just to be the voice for justice. So I would call them to look again, to
examine their points of view and at least to have the will to come and
see alternative ways to deal with this issue.

A WORD TO PILGRIMS

Cedar Duaybis

To Christians thinking of coming to the Holy Land around the
millennium, I would say, come. Of course you should come. This is a
very important event, even we who are familiar with the place and for

whom it has always been our home, we're excited about it. It's not something small that we're celebrating, the two thousandth year of the birth of Jesus, and people are looking forward to it. When many Christians come, it will lift our morale. But I'm always afraid that, after it's over, what then? And if the two thousandth year passes without any improvement in the situation of people here, we've lost an opportunity. So I would say to Christians, don't come only for yourselves, come for us. See us, meet us, discover our situation and do something, not only for the Christians, but for all the people of Palestine. So I would say if they are only coming here to visit and to pray (of course praying is very important) and then to go back and forget us, that will not be good. But if they come and see us and try to help us and stand in solidarity, for a long time after they go back, then that will be very good.

THE SECOND CHRISTMAS AND HOPE

MATTHEW 2:7–11

Then Herod secretly called for the wise men and learned from them the exact time when the star had appeared. Then he sent them to Bethlehem, saying: 'Go and search diligently for the child; and when you have found him, bring me word so that I may also go and pay him homage.' … They set out; and there, ahead of them, went the star that they had seen at its rising, until it stopped over the place where the child was. When they saw that the star had stopped, they were overwhelmed with joy. On entering the house, they saw the child with Mary his mother; and they knelt down and paid him homage. Then, opening their treasure chests, they offered him gifts of gold, frankincense, and myrrh.

Herod is threatened. It is strange how the birth of a little baby can threaten a man of power, and the contrast between the wise men from the east, who are wise enough to kneel before a little child, and the foolish man of power, who resorts once again to brutality, is an obvious one in this passage. To the wise men God gives a further revelation that they should return by a different route. They, of course, are transformed by their visit to Bethlehem and those of us who in humility kneel before the child of Bethlehem, will find that we, too, are changed.

In later church history, people began to call these three wise men 'kings', perhaps to indicate that the kings bow before the King of Kings, or that they are good, wise kings as opposed to a foolish king such as Herod.

Dietrich Bonhoeffer, in prison at the hands of Hitler—another 'Herod'—recognized the enormous significance of this birth at Bethlehem and the way it challenges and changes each one of us.

If God chooses Mary as his instrument, if God himself wants to come into this world in the manger at Bethlehem, that is no idyllic family affair, but the beginning of a complete turnaround, a reordering of everything on this earth. If we wish to take part in this Advent and Christmas event, then we cannot simply be bystanders or onlookers, as if we were at the theatre, enjoying all the cheerful images. No, we ourselves are swept up into the action there, into this conversion of all things. We have to play our part too on this stage, for the spectator is already an actor. We cannot withdraw. What part, then, do we play? Pious shepherds, on bended knee? Kings who come bearing gifts? What sort of play is this, where Mary becomes the mother of God? Where God enters the world in the lowliness of the manger? The judgment of the world and its redemption—that is taking place here. And the Christ child in the manger is himself the one who pronounces the judgment and the redemption of the world. He repels the great and the powerful. He puts down the mighty from their thrones, he humbles the arrogant, his arm overpowers all the proud and the strong, he raises what is lowly and makes it great and splendid in his compassion. Therefore we cannot approach his manger as if it were the cradle of any other child. Those who wish to come to his manger find that something is happening within them.

For the mighty ones, for the great ones in this world, there are only two places where their courage deserts them, which they fear in the depths of their souls, which they dodge and avoid: the manger and the cross of Jesus Christ.

Dietrich Bonhoeffer, *Werke* Vol. 9, London 1933–1935, Goedeking, Heimbucher and Schleicher, 1994, © The Crossroad Publishing Company

Take time to dwell on what the birth in the manger at Bethlehem means for you. What is happening within you—we too are actors, not spectators, and we too are faced with the God of Bethlehem who calls us to turn and follow a humble way of life.

VOICES FROM GAZA ON HOPE

First voice: Suhaila Tarazi

Suhaila Tarazi, the Director of the Ahli Arab Hospital in Gaza (which is a Christian hospital run by the Anglican Diocese of Jerusalem) is an Orthodox Christian. When I asked her if she celebrated Christmas on 7 January she said:

Yes, and I celebrate Christmas every month. I don't have any differentiation! We are all Christians for the one Jesus and I come from a family that believes we are all children of God, whether we are Christian, Muslim or Jew.

She talked about the Bishop of Jerusalem opening the chapel at the Ahli Arab Hospital and said:

He is very open-minded and he opened the church to be used by all, Christians or non-Christians, who would like to come and pray.

She then talked about the current political situation and said:

Peace means changes. Up until this moment we don't feel that there is any change in the life of people and change is very important. As a Christian, I do believe that there will be a candle at the end of the tunnel, but when this candle will be lit is the question. I hope that one day it will be.

Second voice: Costa Dabbagh

Costa Dabbagh is the Director of the Near East Council of Churches which has many projects in Gaza. Costa is also an Orthodox Christian and he says that, on Christmas Eve:

Many would be happy to go and celebrate in Bethlehem, but even though it is part of the PNA territory, we are unable to go there. My daughter is married and lives in Beit Sahour, and she is unable to come here and we are unable to go there. So the two Palestinian National Authority territories, which are supposed to be linked to each other, are separated. We go to church on 7 January but the celebrations are very restricted. People move around and mainly our Muslim neighbours come and greet us at home on that particular day, and then on the following day, we move to other family members and other families of our acquaintance, to say 'Merry Christmas'.

We—like other Christians or Muslims—are unable to reach Jerusalem and there is little joy for the children.

I asked him what hope he saw for the future and he replied:

That's a hard question to answer but as a Christian I feel that hope is always there, in spite of all the difficulties and realities at the moment which do not give us hope. Through our work we try to generate hope for the people, that one day justice will prevail and… our hope will materialize in justice and peace in this region. We follow in the footsteps of Jesus. He had hope and we continue to have the hope that he had. He was crucified at the end, but he had hope that he had saved others by his crucifixion. That is why we follow his determination to spread Christianity.

Third voice: Mahmoud Okshiyya

Mahmoud, a Muslim who works for the Near East Council of Churches, also reflected on hope and said:

We've never lost our hope. Always we have hope, but this time we are more hopeless than at any time before, because of the general situation. I have hope, from the strength of my people, the strength in belief also, and our principles and our rights and so we still continue to have hope. I always want others to be fair.

LET YOUR GENTLENESS BE KNOWN

PHILIPPIANS 4:4–8

Rejoice in the Lord always; again I will say, Rejoice. Let your gentleness be known to everyone. The Lord is near. Do not worry about anything, but in everything by prayer and supplication with thanksgiving let your requests be made known to God. And the peace of God, which surpasses all understanding, will guard your hearts and your minds in Christ Jesus. Finally, beloved, whatever is true, whatever is honourable, whatever is just, whatever is pure, whatever is pleasing, whatever is commendable, if there is any excellence and if there is anything worthy of praise, think about these things.

Our week has been an eye-opener. It was an eye-opener for the wise men who thought that Herod would know where they should be going, and instead they found the answer in the child of Bethlehem. It was an eye-opener for the Samaritan leper who found that his life was made whole and, indeed, an eye-opener for Naaman who, like the wise men, had gone to the king of Israel thinking that was where the answer lay, and instead found that it lay in the prophet Elisha and in the little river Jordan. It's been an eye-opener to two different values, where the weak confound the powerful, where the arrogant are humbled and the lowly are lifted up.

We end the week with this beautiful passage from Paul in Philippians, which reminds us to rejoice constantly in God, and then to let our gentleness be known to everyone. Walter Wink has pointed out how strong 'the myth of redemptive violence' is in our popular culture today, and that the way of Jesus is to reject the domination system. This passage reminds us to be people of a gentle spirit and a humble attitude. It is also a reminder to be those who are not overcome by worry, but who find prayer to be a natural way of communicating with God—prayer that does not forget the aspects of thanksgiving. The result of this way of life will be peace which surpasses all understanding—words which we often use as a blessing. Maybe in these words there is the reminder to simplify our lifestyles so that we do not have to worry about so much—so that we have time for lives that reflect this gentleness and have time for prayer.

Then, finally, Paul reminds us to focus our thoughts and our lives on truth and justice and purity—all things which are pleasing to God—and on those things which are commendable and praise-worthy. Again, if we do these things, we will find that the God of peace is with us. These are wonderful words that are good to meditate on and to repeat regularly.

LIGHTING THE CANDLE

You may want to light several candles today, first one to remember Stephen Lawrence and to pray particularly for Doreen and Neville and their family, a remarkable example of never giving up.

Pray also for the victims of other racial attacks. Light another candle and pray that the demon of racism will be overcome.

Light another candle for the Palestinian community. I recently heard a Palestinian describe his people as the 'un-chosen'. We need to affirm them with the same words that Louise used—you are loved, you are loved. Pray for justice for their community.

Pray also for Jewish people everywhere, who through the centuries have been the victims of racism, and pray that this will never happen again and that they, too, will expunge it from the heart of the state of Israel and link arms with their Semitic sisters and brothers, the Palestinians.

Light a candle for yourself and pray that any subtle prejudice or racism will be removed from your spirit so that we don't think that 'our' group of people is better than another. Try to be honest, and let God's Spirit pluck out your deep prejudices.

Look back at Day 4 (Wednesday) and light a candle and give thanks, and maybe even make a list of all the things for which you would like to thank God. Also spend a little time thinking whether there is someone you ought to thank God for, something they've done which so far you have forgotten about or taken for granted.

EPIPHANY 1 — LOOKING TOWARDS CHRISTMAS 3

Theology for a New Millennium

ZOUGHBI ZOUGHBI:
'EVERY CHURCH IS MY CHURCH'

I am ecumenical, I'm pleased to say. I was baptized Orthodox and I feel every church is my church, and I am a person who believes this. I believe in Jesus Christ our Lord and he is our saviour. I feel all the churches are spotted with the blood of Christ and I belong to each one of the west-east families of churches. I work in the Middle East Council of Churches, which is a very large organization from the churches in the Middle East and this also enhances my ecumenism. Every place I worship, I feel is part of it. When I went to North Carolina, I went to a Baptist church. I felt this was also my church. When I went to England with Christian Aid, I went to an Anglican church as my church. I feel, let's be one, as our Lord wants us to be one. I believe in unity and not uniformity, and I believe in all of the churches.

SUNDAY OF WEEK 7
(Epiphany 1—The Baptism of Christ)

ALL SHALL BE INCLUDED

LUKE 14:12–13, 16–18, 21–23
He said also to the one who had invited him, 'When you give a luncheon or a dinner, do not invite your friends or your brothers or your relatives or rich neighbours, in case they may invite you in return, and you would be repaid. But when you give a banquet, invite the poor, the crippled, the lame, and the blind... Then Jesus said... 'Someone gave a great dinner and invited many. At the time for the dinner he sent his slave to say to those who had been invited, 'Come; for everything is ready now.' But they all alike began to make excuses... Then the owner of the house... said to his slave, 'Go out at once into the streets and lanes of the town and bring in the poor, the crippled, the blind, and the lame.' And the slave said, 'Sir, what you

ordered has been done, and there is still room.' Then the master said to the slave, 'Go out into the roads and lanes, and compel people to come in, so that my house may be filled.'

The idea of a banquet with God is a strong theme in the Old Testament, not only in the Psalms but also in Isaiah 25, where it talks of Yahweh making a banquet for 'all peoples' and for 'all nations'. But Kenneth Bailey points out, in his book *Through Peasant Eyes* (Wm. Eerdman, 1980), that in the inter-testamental period we discover that this image of the banquet becomes less inclusive. It is related to the coming of the Messiah, but the inclusion of Gentiles gets played down and Isaiah's vision is lost. In 1 Enoch 62, the Gentiles suffer punishment and are driven out. In the Qumran community, from which the Dead Sea Scrolls originated, people come to meet the Messiah in ranks: 'First are the judges and officers; then come the chiefs of thousands, fifties, and tens; finally there are the Levites. No one is allowed in who is "smitten in his flesh, or paralysed in his feet and hands, or lame, or blind, or deaf, or dumb, or smitten in his flesh with a visible blemish". All Gentiles are obviously excluded and, along with them, all imperfect Jews' (Kenneth Bailey). So Isaiah's great vision has been watered down—Enoch has had the Gentiles excluded and the Qumran community rejects Jewish unrighteous and those with any physical blemish. Jesus is reflecting an invitation that is exactly the opposite. In other words, bring in the poor, the crippled, the blind and the lame, or as Luke put it earlier, 'Some are last who will be first, and some are first who will be last.'

We now come to the section of excuses which are clearly excuses that don't stand up, particularly when one looks at the culture of the time—indeed they are an insult to the host. In the parable, those who are invited—presumably the leaders of the religious community—are told that the feast is now ready, but they reject the great banquet which has been offered and promised by God in Isaiah. Consequently the host now invites those who are normally ostracized from community life: they are the outcasts of Israel, who have already been attracted to Jesus. The last invitation to those in the 'roads and lanes' seems to refer to the Gentiles and the need to compel them, as in the Middle East custom they would assume that the invitation was not for them—

they would be considered as lower rank. Kenneth Bailey says, though, 'The unexpected guest may be half starving and in real need of the offered food, but still he senses a deep cultural pressure to refuse.'

So Jesus turns upside-down accepted cultural norms and yet is going back to the Isaiah picture of the great banquet which is for all peoples and all nations, and particularly welcomes those who are normally considered as outcast. So all are to be invited into the community of God, and our communion meals should be reflections of this banquet. This is the point at which divisions break down, the point at which the inclusiveness of God's reign should be clearly visible. There are so many things which exclude people within society—class, rank, even religion. Jesus is throwing salvation open to all as an example of God's generosity and grace, and the last shall be first: the marginalized, the poor, the forgotten, the outcasts, are welcomed into God's kingdom first. Others are not excluded unless they want to be excluded; they too can come, but it may well be a humbling experience when they recognize that they come without their rank and status. This is why kneeling before the communion table is such a significant moment: it is where everyone is equal, where the poor are lifted up and the powerful must be humble.

What a wonderfully inclusive community it is that both Isaiah and Jesus envisage. Do our churches reflect this? This parable has huge implications for how we live. Will we continue to issue the invitation that should be offered by those of the community of God? Will we allow our lives to be lived in the same way, including all, or will we commit ourselves to a lifestyle that excludes many and offers them no good news?

It is strange how this inclusive image is often unpopular, so that the writers of the inter-testamental period had to obscure Isaiah's vision. As we saw earlier, when Jesus spoke in the synagogue in Nazareth, what he said was perfectly acceptable until he suggested that it was no longer an exclusive message, and at this point they were 'filled with rage' and tried to throw him off the brow of the hill. Jesus does not bring a reign that is comfortable. We would rather have a church that is more like a club—that has membership of the 'right sort' of people. But Jesus says that those days are over: the excluded are now included, the last shall be first, but the first will also be there, though last. So the powerful and the rich and those with status are not forgotten, they are simply shown the road of humility—then they are welcome too.

PRAYER
O God, you promise a world
Where those who now weep shall laugh,
Those who are hungry shall feast
Those who are poor now, and excluded,
Shall have your kingdom for their own.

I want this world too.
I renounce despair.
I will act for change.
I choose to be included
In your great feast of life.
Christian Aid Prayer of Commitment

MONDAY OF WEEK 7

THE COMMUNITY OF JESUS

LUKE 16:19–26
'There was a rich man who was dressed in purple and fine linen and who feasted sumptuously every day. And at his gate lay a poor man named Lazarus, covered with sores, who longed to satisfy his hunger with what fell from the rich man's table... The poor man died and was carried away by the angels to be with Abraham. The rich man also died and was buried. In Hades, where he was being tormented, he looked up and saw Abraham far away with Lazarus by his side. He called out, "Father Abraham, have mercy on me, and send Lazarus to dip the tip of his finger in water and cool my tongue; for I am in agony." But Abraham said, "Child, remember that during your lifetime you received your good things, and Lazarus in like manner evil things; but now he is comforted here, and you are in agony. Besides all this, between you and us a great chasm has been fixed... and no one can cross from there to us."'

I have called this week 'Theology for a New Millennium' partly because I'm constantly haunted by the vision of Christianity going into religious fervour a thousand years ago, resulting in the horror of the Crusades. We also have to face the terrible problem of what Christians have done to Jews through the last two millennia, and on our journey to Bethlehem we cannot ignore the three religious players in this part of the world—Muslim, Jew and Christian—and the fact that our history is intertwined with violence. For Jew and Christian, we have to address that violence in our own scriptures and, in turn, the history of this part of the world, which has seen aggression and invasion, and people being driven from their homes and turned into refugees.

Sometimes the attempt of one religion to gain ascendancy over another group of people or faith community has been strong in history—we see it in Jerusalem at the moment. There is an attempt to make it the city of one group of people, and yet the only hope, so that history does not repeat itself with all its violence, is that, as Yehezkel Landau puts it, 'Parts have to be sacrificed for the common blessing.' Our great visions for our people, for our community or our religion, must sometimes be sacrificed for a greater vision which builds an inclusive community where sharing brings hope. As Jewish theologian, Marc Ellis, has put it, 'There is a need to reject the Constantinian or Empire view of religion, which is a temptation within all faiths, and rather to go for the community aspect, i.e. serving rather than dominating.'

Today's reading reflects another of the divisions in our world which requires a response. Deep imbalances are not new, and Jesus is reminding us to take the opportunity to serve the poor and to heal this awful division between rich and poor while we can.

As Jon Sobrino says:

In modern western cultures, even those with a religious basis, it becomes even more difficult to keep to the first commandment: 'You shall not worship false gods.' As Jesus says, 'No man can serve two masters, God and riches.' With that we are back to the origin of sin: stealing. When we accumulate riches, we are gradually or violently depriving other human beings, our brothers and sisters, of life. Expressed more strongly, we are bringing death.
From *Passion For Justice*, CAFOD/Darton, Longman and Todd, 1997

The Old Testament prophets had repeatedly taken up the theme of doing justice and showing mercy, and the parable ends with the rather negative thought that people have not listened to Moses and the prophets, nor will they be convinced if someone rises from the dead.

Perhaps this is where the role of the Church comes in: to be a community that brings life and not only listens, but is constantly challenging its members to be those who listen, to be this alternative community.

Journeying with Jesus also means to be in a community; to become part of the alternative community of Jesus. Discipleship is not an individual path, but a journey in a company of disciples. It is the road less travelled, yet discipleship involves being in a community that remembers and celebrates Jesus. Though that is not the only role of the church, it is its primary role. To use John Shea's very apt description of the church, 'Gather the folks, tell the stories, break the bread.' Discipleship involves being compassionate. 'Be compassionate as God is compassionate' is the defining mark of the followers of Jesus. Compassion is the fruit of life in the Spirit and the ethos of the community of Jesus.

Marcus J. Borg, *Meeting Jesus Again For The First Time*, HarperCollins Inc., 1994

PRAYER
Almighty and everlasting God, you have revealed the incarnation of your Son by the bright shining of a star, which led the wise men to offer costly gifts in adoration. Let the star of your justice give light to our hearts, that we may give as our treasure all that we possess and all that we are; through Jesus Christ our Lord.

Gelasian, from *The Promise of his Glory*, Church House Publishing

MITRI RAHEB ON HOPE AND SACRIFICE

How can you hold to hope, when the hope longed for seems to be shattered? The critical moment in Palestine today is this, that the majority of Palestinians, but also a great number of Israelis, have lost their hope. They cannot dream any more, it seems there is nothing to dream about, nothing to hope for, nothing to long for. In the context of this hopelessness, we hear about people killed in Palestine, Cambodia, Sudan, Somalia and Kosovo...

We do not sacrifice bulls and goats any more. Humans are more sophisticated today. For what we sacrifice today is human beings— children and many people are sacrificed every day on the altar of nationhood, statehood, and national and religious ambitions and myths... and those who don't sacrifice their own people still produce and sell weapons so that others might sacrifice.

IS ANYONE LISTENING?

JAMES 1:19–20, 22, 27

You must understand this, my beloved: let everyone be quick to listen, slow to speak, slow to anger; for your anger does not produce God's righteousness... But be doers of the word, and not merely hearers who deceive themselves... Religion that is pure and undefiled before God, the Father, is this: to care for orphans and widows in their distress, and to keep oneself unstained by the world.

Being quick to listen could not be more important. So often we are not quick to listen to the other point of view, but rather we are quick to speak. But here in the letter of James very good advice is given— 'be listening people, and slow to anger'—and here there is a contrast between listening and hearing. Listening means understanding but too often we haven't listened and understood. Here we are challenged by God to listen, to understand and to act—to be 'doers of the word'. This is true and pure religion which gets reflected in action, for example, in caring for orphans and widows.

Peacemaker and Greek Melkite priest, Elias Chacour, has set up a 'listening post' in his school up at Ibillin in Galilee. His concern is that people should listen to each other's stories first and that this will help understanding and help each group to get inside the mind of the other, so that they go forward together. It is a remarkable monument and perhaps at the moment unique, though we hope that it will not remain so for long. Elias says this of the 'listening post':

The listening post is my personal Holocaust monument, the first Palestinian Holocaust monument, and this is represented by two semi-circular walls facing each other and forming a full circle. On each of these walls there is a statement, one in Arabic and one in Hebrew, for the Jews and for the Arabs. In Arabic it says, 'This is a memorial for Jewish martyrs' and in Hebrew it says, 'This is a memorial for Palestinian martyrs' and on the outside, on the other side of the walls, is written, carved in concrete, 'listening post'. It is saying, 'Come and listen to the martyrs.' I think they jointly say 'enough martyrs'. Then this is a reminder that the martyrs of one side are viewed as terrorists on the other side. Our responsibility is first to stop producing martyrs and then to honour our martyrs. In this way we can work together towards a better future, rather than buying weapons—weapons that not only kill the body but weapons that kill the spirit, that kill the reputation, that kill dignity and self-esteem...

It was inspired from an invitation I received when I was in Washington at the State Apartment. I was invited to visit the Jewish Holocaust monument in Washington DC which is much bigger and much wealthier than the White House itself. I did not want to go there and I told my hosts, all the time there is no mention of the Palestinian Holocaust and other human Holocausts. I see no need and no sense to go and visit one of the Holocausts in order to remember—and to avoid others... That's a very strange attitude that can create everything except friendship.

Elias has spent time, along with a survivor of the Jewish Holocaust, in Cambodia, speaking of his experiences to those who were traumatized by, yet survived, the days of the 'killing fields'. His concern is that we should listen to the pain of all holocausts and learn from them, so we do not repeat them. Later this week we will hear of the pain of the Armenians, who suffered a holocaust which is largely forgotten.

PRAYER: 'YOU TEACH ME TO LISTEN, JESUS'
You teach me to listen, Jesus;
I hear the cry of the victims
Of Auschwitz and Belsen.
I see the grief in the faces
Of those who lost family and friends
In the Holocaust

And I pray that your people, the Jews,
May have security and peace.

You teach me to listen, Jesus;
I hear the cry of the victims
Of Sabra and Shatila.
I see the grief in the faces
Of mothers who lost their children
In the Intifada.
I pray that your people, the Palestinians,
May have justice and peace.

Holy God, I seek to listen with both ears,
To hear the cry of the Israelites
To hear the cry of the Palestinians
And to be a friend to both communities
Praying that both may know your love and peace.

John Johansen-Berg, from *Seeing Christ in Others*, ed. Geoffrey Duncan,
Canterbury Press, 1998

Voices from Jericho on Hope

First voice: Randa Hilal

Each day Randa Hilal, the Director of the Jericho YMCA Vocational
Training Centre in Jericho, has to travel for forty minutes from her
home in Ramallah to get to her work. Sometimes it can take even
longer because of the closures and, on occasions, it will be very
difficult and take several hours. The YMCA Training Centre is a place
of hope, and Randa comments:

*The centre is a hopeful place. You find a lot of desperate people coming to us
with very bad social and economical hardship. At the end of their training
they can find jobs and can support themselves and their families. Some of
them even have their own workshops or have their own business after they
finish. We have students from all over Palestine who are benefiting from this
work, but we mainly target the needy people, putting emphasis also on
woman and on the handicapped, and special-needs people. As well as training
students, we also train adults in new technology and new developments.*

We used to have students from Gaza up until 1992. After that it was very difficult. At the beginning of the peace process, people told us that we are going to get back all the West Bank and Gaza and we are going to have a flourishing economy and lots of investors would come from abroad. People did start coming, investors started coming, at the beginning of 1994 and 1995, but after that it stopped, and a lot of businesses have been affected. Our students are even crying sometimes over the situation, the economic situation and the lack of hope. I wish and I hope that we could get peace because it's the only solution.

Randa is an Orthodox Christian, so I asked her when she celebrated Christmas.

We used to celebrate on 7 January, but in Ramallah and other places, after the Palestinian Authority came, they decided to unify all the feasts, so you find that they all celebrate Christmas on 25 December, and they celebrate Easter on the eastern feast. At Christmas time in Ramallah, we have a very big Scout event that day. My children are part of this, and it's very interesting, and they move all around Ramallah. They get Scouts from different parts, and they get together and go around the streets for three hours on the 24th and in the evening we have a celebration, and invite relations and friends.

On 6 January evening, I still go to Bethlehem, because they have the service there and there are less people than on 24 December. Here in the Centre, we celebrate Christmas with the students. We do the Christmas tree and we have some celebration with songs and acting and we give them a dinner.

Second voice: Sami Musallam

Dr Sami Musallam, Director General of the President's Office in Jericho, and a member of the Palestinian National Authority, came originally from Jerusalem, where he studied at the Lutheran Evangelical School before going on to various universities. Now, as Director of the Office of President Arafat in Jericho, which is one of the President's official seats, he has considerable responsibility within the PNA. He is also head of the Committee for the Promotion of Tourism. He is concerned that the Palestinians should not lose hope.

We should not lose hope, because if we lose hope, we lose the meaning of our existence. We think that the majority of the Israeli public wants peace, but this large minority in the Israeli public who do not want to make peace or reconcile with the Palestinian people, and with the other Arab peoples, make themselves heard...

How long can people bear the very difficult conditions which are reaching the level of poverty in all the Palestinian Territories? Unemployment rates have soared up and the standard of living has dropped.

Still I don't want to lose hope. I'm working so that we do not lose hope, because if we lose hope it will be a very dim future...

Palestine is a very beautiful country. It is also historic. The history of humankind is almost summarized in this little country, and it provides tourism for all kinds of people. For those believers who want to celebrate the second millennium of the birth of Jesus Christ this is the only place where Jesus Christ was born, lived, and was crucified. Here in Palestine you find the one Holy Sepulchre. In Bethlehem is the one Church of the Nativity where Jesus Christ was born. There is only one Mount of Temptation and that's in Jericho. So this is a place for pilgrims, but also for everyone. For those who are interested in eco-tourism, this is the most beautiful area for eco-tourism—for those interested in historical tourism, the country is full of archeological sites.

We hope that the creation of the Palestinian State on the land of Palestine will coincide with the second millennium. As we celebrate the birth of Jesus Christ and remember the message of Jesus Christ's resurrection, we hope it will be the resurrection of a people who have been trodden upon throughout the previous century. It took this people, the Palestinian people, around one century of resistance in order to get its rebirth, so the message of rebirth and the message of resurrection can very beautifully apply to the Palestinian people.

WEDNESDAY OF WEEK 7

IN THE NAME OF GOD

JOSHUA 6:2–5, 16–17, 21, 24–25, 27 (ABRIDGED)

The Lord said to Joshua, 'See, I have handed Jericho over to you. You shall march around the city. Thus you shall do for six days. On the seventh day you shall march around the city seven times, the priests

blowing the trumpets, then all the people shall shout with a great shout; and the wall of the city will fall down flat...' And at the seventh time, Joshua said to the people, 'Shout! For the Lord has given you the city. The city and all that is in it shall be devoted to the Lord for destruction.' ... Then they devoted to destruction by the edge of the sword all in the city, both men and women, young and old, oxen, sheep, and donkeys... They burned down the city, and everything in it. But Rahab the prostitute, with her family and all who belonged to her, Joshua spared... So the Lord was with Joshua...

Jericho, the city of palms, is a beautiful place and it is one of the places I most enjoy visiting when I come to this part of Palestine. Many coaches simply rush straight to Tel Jericho (or Tell es-Sultan), which is the location of the oldest city at Jericho, and often bypass the very atmospheric, sleepy little square in modern Jericho. Here it is very pleasant to stroll around looking at the stalls and the shops and soaking in the atmosphere of one of the first cities of emerging Palestine. Several times I have been to the Holy Land in winter and have fled to Jericho from Jerusalem to get warm!

The story of Joshua taking the city is a difficult one. It is certainly not supported by archeological finds and the whole tenure of the invasion of Joshua, with the insistence by God that everyone must be killed, is very problematic. The story probably comes from the post-exilic period and perhaps reflects a concern of the writer to strengthen the sense of exclusivity of the people of Israel, and the fact that God was on their side. The book of Judges, written at the same time, certainly shows a different picture as to how the land became occupied. Sadly, later groups, such as the crusaders or the Christians who invaded Latin America and put into action many other colonial exercises, have justified what they have done using the same terminology and with reference to this Old Testament invasion. It happened in apartheid South Africa, it happens today when Jewish settlers use the same justification, and it should encourage us to come to grips with the character of God.

What sort of God is it that we follow and that we find revealed in the Bible? The Bible is certainly a journey in our understanding of God. As the Hebrew scriptures go on further, they come to the remarkable picture of God in Isaiah which, as we have already seen, reflects an inclusive view. This, too, is the way of Jesus. Perhaps it is easier to see it clearly if we look at where we end up if we take the other view. Maybe like Yigal Amir, who after killing Prime Minister Yitzhak Rabin, claimed that he had done it 'in the name of God'. The question that springs to mind is, in the name of which God?

IN THE NAME OF GOD

He shot down a man of peace
In the name of God
Shot down a man of peace
In the name of God

So how will the hatred cease
How will the bloodshed cease
If you kill all those of peace
In the name of God

Centuries of cruelty
In the name of God
Wars of religion
In the name of God
So who is this vengeful God
Demanding so much blood
I'm learning to dread the words
In the name of God

In the name of God what have we done
In the name of God where will it end
In the name of God lay down our guns
In the name of God
In the name of God let's share the land
In the name of God hold someone's hand
In the name of God let's take a stand
For love

What kind of God is this, what kind of God is this
Who demands such a bloody kiss as an act of love
Is there another God who calls for a way of love

Where we don't have to dominate—to hate or to kill
Is there another God who calls us to serve and love
Love our neighbour as ourself in the name of God

Garth Hewitt, © Chain of Love music

ROCK 'N' ROLL EXILE

The last person to embrace Prime Minister Yitzak Rabin and bid him *Shalom* (peace), a mere ten minutes before he was gunned down, was the singer, Aviv Geffen. He is one of Israel's biggest-selling artists, but is currently in exile in Britain. He says, 'I'm just 24 and I came face-to-face with death... With three bullets Amir killed both a very brave man and the peace.' Committed to peace, Geffen says of extremists, 'The Bible belongs to me as well as to them... I've become a symbol of modern Israel... I'm holding the flag for weakness. Let's cry and write about the tears... My weapon is my pen... I believe in a God of love.'

THURSDAY OF WEEK 7

LOVE YOUR ENEMIES

LUKE 6:27–28, 31, 33–36

'Love your enemies, do good to those who hate you, bless those who curse you, pray for those who abuse you... Do to others as you would have them do to you... If you do good to those who do good to you, what credit is that to you? ... If you lend to those from whom you hope to receive, what credit is that to you? Even sinners lend to sinners, to receive as much again. But love your enemies, do good, and lend, expecting nothing in return. Your reward will be great, and you will be children of the Most High... Be merciful, just as your Father is merciful.'

The words 'Do to others as you would have them do to you' have sometimes been called the Golden Rule. These words, along with 'Love your enemies and do good to those who hate you', are a key to our behaviour. In the United States at the moment there is a fashion accessory—a bracelet that you can buy—which has on it the initials

'WWJD'. The letters stand for 'What Would Jesus Do?' Good as that is as an idea, it can be a little vague if we are not familiar with the teachings and the actions of Jesus. One could start to 'justify' all sorts of behaviour with the supposed example of Jesus. The Golden Rule, however, turns things round to make sure we put ourselves in the place of other people, and this is very much the teaching of Jesus— saying, 'Behave to others as you would like them to behave to you.' We would like people to be merciful to us, we would like them to lend to us, we would like them to love us, and so Jesus says, do that to others, and do it even to your enemies.

In our journey towards Bethlehem, through the lands of Palestine and Israel, we find many people who cannot talk to one another. One group is oppressed by another group; one group uses brutality to another. These words of love for enemy and of the Golden Rule are the basis for a true and lasting peace. As Naim Ateek says, 'The genuine answers to peace lie in everything that the child of Bethlehem has stood for: humility, openness, love of others, forgiveness, even sacrifice of oneself for others.' So, as well as a geographical journey to Bethlehem, there is a symbolic one in which we see that the hope for the future and the hope for the road of peace begin with the humility and the love even of enemies, and that this begins in a manger in Bethlehem. It is a humble road. It is accepting Christ like a little child, rather than like a dominating, arrogant person. It is listening to the other person. It is putting oneself in the other person's shoes. If we behave in this way, we will be considered as children of the Most High.

One of the key attributes of God, a viewpoint that is common to Christianity, Islam and Judaism, is that God is merciful, and therefore we should be merciful. Today's words could not be more important.

On our journey towards Bethlehem we have visited many peace-makers, who have often done simple yet courageous things to make a stand for peace. On a Friday in Jerusalem, there is a group of mainly Jewish women called the Women in Black who stand round a square in west Jerusalem with signs, and campaign silently for peace. They receive abuse. While I was standing there one Friday interviewing them, our interview was interrupted several times by yells. But they stand there as a silent witness, to say that there is a better way. Interestingly, two out of the three that I interviewed were not religious people and I was surprised, on my most recent journey, that several people I met from different religions had given up on religion because of the conflict it causes. Yet if we look at these words and the true living out of the heart of the teaching of Jesus, then religion need not be rejected. It can be a partner in the process to peace. Mahatma Gandhi's view that if only Christians would have followed the way of Jesus, he would have become a Christian, is an ongoing challenge to us. Again, these words give us the measure by which to live our lives.

PRAYER
God of peace, merciful God, teach us to do unto others as we would have them do unto us. Amen

VOICES OF HOPE FROM THE WOMEN IN BLACK

First voice: Nomi Morag
The first 'Woman in Black' I spoke to was Nomi Morag, who is Jewish and lives in Jerusalem but was born in a kibbutz in Upper Galilee. She has stood as part of the silent protest in Jerusalem for the last ten years.

Unfortunately, ten years have passed and nothing has really changed… The only thing I can do, instead of sitting in my house and lecturing everybody about how peace is necessary, is to stand here… My parents are Holocaust survivors and they could do nothing at that time… I was always raised up on the idea that I was a part of the victim people, and all of a sudden I'm not… and the only thing I could do was to come here and protest in silence. This is the licence that we have, to stand here without shouting, without marching, just to stand.

We got the idea from the women in Argentina, where the mothers of the disappeared were standing every week with the pictures of their sons and loved ones. It was a silent demonstration. I think it's the best thing. I mean, what can I say? Nothing. It's just me standing here with the sign… My son is in the army, he's a conscript soldier and has just came down from Lebanon after staying there for about five months, which was a terrible time, so I feel that I have to be here.

I went to Tel Aviv one day and I saw graffiti on the wall, which said, 'We too wanted to have a state once', and that was very, very powerful to me because it really is what happened fifty years ago. We were in a position where we were refugees from all over the world coming here. We didn't have a state… and we had to fight. It was a fight for our survival. So every means to achieve this goal was considered OK.

I asked her if she still had a flicker of hope.

Always, otherwise I wouldn't stand here. I have children, and I want them to live in this country… This is the only country I have, I was born here and so were my parents. I have to fight for this country, to fight for its democracy, for its proper ruling, proper government, uncorrupted government, and peace and justice and everything that I believe in. I can't just sit at home and do nothing, and whine about it.

Second voice: Gila Svirsky

Gila Svirsky is also Jewish and is the Director of Bat Shalom, a women's peace organization in Israel.

My real push toward activism came with Women in Black in 1988 when the Intifada began.

I asked her if she was hopeful at all for the future.

You have to be hopeful. When you look around and take a long view of things, you see that there has been progress…

My hope for the future is that, in the short run, we will have two states—the state of Palestine side by side with the state of Israel—each one autonomous, each one able to grow and develop in its own way, with free trade and free commerce between the two. My hope for the long run is that there will no longer be states and nationalism in the world and we'll all live as one big happy family.

Third voice: Marylene Schultz

Marylene Schultz, who is French by nationality and a Christian, lived in Jordan from 1967. Now she lives with the Palestinians, and says:

I think occupation is destroying people, both the occupier and the occupied. For me it's very difficult to say we can do nothing. For me as a non-Jew it's very important that I meet with Jewish people who are not soldiers, so that I don't need to be afraid of them… I am part of the Palestinian people now and I think it's very easy to become anti-Israeli, but I don't want to be, so to have contact with these women is important, and this helps me.

Fourth voice: Ohro

Some of our Amos Collective group dressed in black and joined the protest when we were there in February. Later, Katie Goulborn told me the story of the woman who had stood next to her—we don't know her full name but her first name was Ohro. Katie told me that Ohro is Jewish and one of the fifteen people who go and protest every week. For her it's the worst day as she is preparing for the Sabbath, but that is part of her sacrifice. Ohro said to Katie that the thing that really angered her was the way that most of the men treat them like 'silly little women who don't understand about politics'.

Katie asked her if she thought many Israelis supported what she did, and she said she felt there was a silent majority who think that what she is doing is very good, but they won't get up and do it themselves. She is a very strong practising Jew, and she always makes sure she's prepared for the Sabbath before going to protest.

FRIDAY OF WEEK 7

'NO PEOPLE' BECOME 'GOD'S PEOPLE'

1 PETER 2:10
Once you were not a people, but now you are God's people; once you had not received mercy, but now you have received mercy.

The focus of Christian Aid Week in May 1997 was on India, and in particular on some of our partners in the church of south India, especially the Dalits of India. The Dalits used to be called the untouchables or, by Gandhi, the harijans (the children of God). The word 'Dalit' was chosen by the Dalits themselves and means the broken, scattered, downtrodden, crushed, and destroyed. There are four castes in Hindu society in the Varna system, and then come the Avarnas or outcasts—'no people'. Though technically illegal, discrimination against Dalits is still practised.

On visits to India I have met various Dalits and heard their stories. In 1997, as we had the focus on India, several Christian Aid partners came over who were Dalits, and who reminded me again of both their situation and how they view God. They talk of 'no people' becoming 'God's people' and how the gospel has liberated them and brought them to dignity and hope.

A.P. Nirmal is an Indian Dalit theologian who has written a paper with the title, 'From no people to God's people'. He talks not only about the meaning of the word Dalit, but how the Christian Dalit community, in the first phase of mass conversions, moved to Christ because they were tired of inhuman and unjust treatment and wanted a viable alternative. They were looking for a religion that would give them a sense of dignity as human beings. They converted as families and communities and they are now the backbone of the Indian church. Possibly as many as 85 per cent of the Christian church in India are Dalits and the Indian church has at least 18 million people. In Indian society as a whole, there are about 200 million Dalits.

A.P. Nirmal points out that Dalit Christians identify with two aspects of God which are reflected in Jesus: one, the God who suffers and, two, the God who serves. He says:

The God who we know through our suffering is the God who suffers like ourselves. Our own experience of suffering unites us with this suffering God. Our God is a Dalit deity. The suffering servant of Isaiah 53 thus became a helpful concept of God for the Dalits.

And about the God who serves, he says:

The other aspect that connects us with this suffering servant is the idea of servanthood of God. The life of the Indian Dalits is characterized by their servitude. We therefore find the concept of the servant God meaningful and relevant, thus suffering and service are united in our God.

A.P. Nirmal feels that God's glory is displayed and manifested as he identifies with the weak and the oppressed, the downtrodden and the crushed, and as he brings them salvation, redemption and liberation, and when he leads no people to be God's people.

In the introduction to a book called *The Palestinian Nakba* (*nakba* means 'catastrophe') published by the Palestinian Return Centre in London, it says of the Palestinian community:

At the fiftieth anniversary of their Holocaust, this Register is an attempt to put in print what is already engraved in the minds and hearts of millions of refugees. This Register is a part of an ongoing project to document the collective memory of the 'unchosen' but determined people.

I had not heard Palestinians describe themselves in that way before—but being 'unchosen' is not dissimilar from being 'no people'. The particular difficulty for the Palestinians is that often it is religious people from Christian or Jewish communities who are telling them they are 'unchosen, 'they are 'no people'. Yet these words at the beginning of our passage today remind us that the new covenant is open to all: 'no people' find their meaning and become God's people.

Faith can be used to exclude and oppress and dehumanize, or it can be used to allow people to capture the vision of their full worth and to find their humanity and their dignity. The 'unchosen' find that indeed they are chosen. 'No people' become God's people.

This is because brokenness belongs to the very being of God. God is one with broken people, the Dalit people. God suffers when God's people suffer. God weeps when God's people weep. God laughs when God's people laugh. God dies when God's people die. And God rises again in God's people's resurrection.

A.P. Nirmal

THE ARMENIANS AND THE THIRD CHRISTMAS

One group of people who were treated as 'no people' and lost their land were the Armenians. In 1915 they experienced an attempted genocide in which over one and a half million of their people disappeared. It started when the Turkish police in Constantinople, on 24 April 1915, rounded up three hundred prominent Armenians—members of parliament, clergymen, writers and artists. Simultaneously, thousands of Armenian intellectuals were arrested in all the cities of Turkey and sent to their deaths. In the months of April, May and June, about two million Armenians were forcibly deported from Ottoman Turkey and a horrendous series of massacres then occurred.

When I was in Jerusalem in August 1998 for the enthronement of Bishop Riah Abu el-Assal, I spent some time walking round the Armenian quarter. There were posters and maps on display giving information about the Armenian genocide. I also met up with the Armenian Patriarch, Archbishop Torkom Manoogian, and he very kindly sent me three books of Armenian music, which are absolutely fascinating. Evidently, the best Armenian musician is a man called Gomidas Vartabed and the Archbishop has written a short history of his songs. Something of the beauty of Armenian culture comes out in all of this, and the pain and the yearning for what was lost.

The Armenians celebrate Christmas on 19 January, and through the words of one or two Armenian Christians we will discover a little bit more about their story as we look to the third Christmas that's celebrated. First, Father Sahag Mashalian, an Armenian Orthodox priest in Jerusalem, explains why they celebrate Christmas on this date.

Nowadays when the Christmas season ends worldwide by 6 January, Armenian Orthodox celebrations in Bethlehem on 18 and 19 January may seem odd... We do not know the exact date of Christ's birth, since no date is given in the Gospels. Historically speaking, though, we may safely assert that 6 January was the oldest date of the celebration in all the churches.

Theophany, the manifestation (Greek: epiphaneia) of God to the world in Jesus Christ is first known to have been honoured in the third century on 6 January. There is certain evidence that this festival may be older. Egeria Silvia of Bordeaux, whose writings about her pilgrimage to the Holy Land in 385 have recently been discovered, testifies that 6 January was observed in Bethlehem as the feast day of Christ's birth. A letter directed to the Bishop of Rome in the fourth century gives valuable detail on how these celebrations took place:

The faithful met before dawn at Bethlehem to celebrate the birth from the Virgin in the cave; but before their hymns and the prayers were over they had to hurry off to the River Jordan (thirteen miles away) to celebrate the baptism. The consequence was that neither commemoration could be kept fully and properly... The change to 25 December, along with the establishment of a new Christian festival called Christmas or Nativity, happened in the West in the fourth century. 25 December was the date of a pagan festival in Rome, chosen in 274 by the emperor Aurelin as the birthday of the unconquered sun... which begins to show an increase of light at the winter solstice. At some point before 336, the church in Rome established the commemoration of the birthday of Christ, the Sun of Righteousness, on the same date. The prevailing Christian festival, Theophany, was divided into two: the birth of Christ with the name of Christmas on 25 December and the baptism and the visitation of the magi with the name of Epiphany on 6 January.

The Armenian church did not follow the change and clung to the older date and form. This was for various reasons. Armenia was not within the Roman Empire. Armenians did not have such a pagan festival on 25 December to suppress, so it did not see any reason to follow the new custom. The rest of the Eastern churches use the old Julian calendar instead of the Gregorian calendar. There is a difference of thirteen days between these two calendars, which explains why the Armenian celebrations in Bethlehem take place at such a late date, on 19 January and not 6 January.

We must highlight the fact that liturgy and festivals are not merely memorial celebrations of past events but actual participation in a continual truth... Our church calendar is an eternal journey that we walk through again and again with Jesus Christ, living his thirty-three earthly years of ministry until his return.

This is a song from one of the books that Archbishop Torkom Manoogian gave me.

It is not the sun that lights the world,
Gives nature its beauty, colour and life.
It is not the stars that endow the sky
With nocturnal grace found nowhere else.

The torch that sparks all other lights
From which the grace of all things flares
—Without it the world is lifeless and dark—
Is the joy of the soul that loves and cares.

Song Of Joy by Schahan Barberian

THREE CHRISTMASES ARE BETTER THAN ONE!

Cedar Duaybis

I don't mind the three Christmases. There are many Christians who think unity comes if we have just one celebration. No, I actually enjoy having three because I can celebrate my own Christmas and then go and have time for the Greek Orthodox and the Armenians. I don't mind it at all. Three Christmases are better than one!

SATURDAY OF WEEK 7

LOOKING FORWARD... TO THE THIRD CHRISTMAS

JOHN 1:10, 12, 14, 18

He was in the world, and the world came into being through him; yet the world did not know him... But to all who received him, who believed in his name, he gave power to become children of God... And the Word became flesh and lived among us, and we have seen his glory, the glory as of a father's only son, full of grace and truth... No one has ever seen God. It is God the only Son, who is close to the Father's heart, who has made him known.

So we end our journey back at Bethlehem again, reminded once more of the birth of Jesus in these beautiful words from the prologue of John's Gospel. John's Gospel was written later than the other Gospels and so there had been a chance to think about the significance of Jesus and his birth, and of John the Baptist, the Elijah figure who came to prepare the way for Jesus. A few verses further on, in verse 23, we find John saying, 'I am the voice of one crying out in the wilderness, "Make straight the way of the Lord" as the prophet Isaiah said.' Not only does John point to the prophecy of Isaiah, he also uses the imagery of Jesus as the 'lamb of God', an image that conjures up the concept of someone who is humble, non-violent and sacrificial.

In the birth, the lifestyle, the death and resurrection of Jesus, we discover something about God's heart and God's character and, in turn, how we should live and, of course, a theology for a new millennium. If this wonderful truth got hijacked when Christianity became the official religion of the Roman Empire, if it is always a struggle between Empire and community—between domination and serving—then maybe it is a good thing that we celebrate three Christmases. These three celebrations take us back again and again to the humility of being born a vulnerable child in a place where there was no room in the inn, in a simple manger. The image of a lamb on the throne, in the book of Revelation, is a significant one that links in with this truth. Jesus is not some all-powerful conquering king, but rather the humble sacrificial lamb. It is this road that we follow to avoid the conflicts and the violence and the mistakes of the previous centuries.

An Armenian Voice for Hope

Nora Karmi is an Armenian Palestinian who works for Sabeel based in east Jerusalem. Her family had lived in the Baka'a neighbourhood of west Jerusalem for many years and left there as refugees during the fighting in 1948. They left with just one suitcase because they were hoping they would be back within a fortnight. Their house and all their possessions were taken and they've never been able to get them back.

Nora told me a little about the Armenian church.

Armenia is the first state that became Christian, in 301. Ever since then, there have been pilgrims and clergy coming into Jerusalem, and many of the saints that were in the deserts in the fifth and sixth centuries were Armenians. There has been a presence of Armenians ever since then in the holy city… Most Armenians, though, came here at the beginning of this century, after 1917, after the genocide. So my roots are indigenous on my mother's side and with my father they came during that period.

Nora then talked about the Armenian traditions within Advent and Christmas.

We have a kind of Vespers—an evening service—every Tuesday and Thursday throughout Advent. As in all Eastern churches, the Gospels are read over and over and we fast throughout that period. In fact, our New Year comes on the 14th, and we are still fasting, so we have specific dishes because we are fasting. Our Christmas comes after New Year, strangely enough, so we break our fast on Christmas Day. We celebrate by going to church in Bethlehem. There is a procession on the 18th in the morning, and then a second service around two o'clock. There is another service around six o'clock, and finally a procession for everybody, and the midnight mass that is televised. Everybody tries to be there in Bethlehem. Our numbers have dwindled to around four thousand Armenian Christians in the West Bank and Israel.

Nora then talked about her hope.

People are feeling strangled. And where do I get my hope? I think it is my faith that gives me the hope. After seeing the support of so many international friends at the Sabeel Conference, I'm sure that many people will go back and try to influence not only the governments but also the churches. I put my hope more on the churches. I think the churches have not done enough to show that this is a just cause. My whole faith is based on the crucifixion and the resurrection and this is the way I see things. I see this as a time when we are suffering the way of the cross, but the way of the cross ends up in hope.

We started our journey using the words 'Come, Lord Jesus' into situations of pain and conflict and hopelessness. Maybe we can echo that prayer once more.

Come, Lord Jesus, bring justice for the Palestinian community, that this land will be shared between Palestinian and Jew in a way that reflects equality and dignity for all, that both communities may live together in justice and in peace.

TO THINK ABOUT
When Hitler was planning the Holocaust he could calmly assert that nobody remembers the Armenians now (Robin Cook, The Observer, 14 June 1998).

LIGHTING THE CANDLE

And what about ourselves? It is a new year, a new century, a new millennium. Let's light a last candle on this journey and thank God for Bethlehem, thank God for the faithful witness through the centuries of the local Christian community, thank God for the people of good will, who even now, against all odds, still want to see the dawning of peace. And for ourselves, let us pray that we have the spirit of Bethlehem, the humility and the hope that are both reflected in this remarkable birth. Also light a candle for the Armenians—victims of a forgotten Holocaust—and pray that no communities will be ignored, and pray that the light and hope of Bethlehem will spread around our world.

Shine on, shine on, star of Bethlehem
Shine as on that night
Shine on, shine on, star of Bethlehem
Teach us to show your light
Garth Hewitt, © Chain of Love Music

PRAYER

Lord God, we have journeyed with you through Advent, three celebrations of Christmas, the New Year and Epiphany. We have waited and watched. We have prayed, 'Come, Lord Jesus.' We have lit candles of hope. We have heard the voice of the prophets of old who are signposts of hope.

As we came to the longest night of the year, Jesus led us from darkness to light. We have walked into a new year with all the hope of new beginnings. Your extraordinary message, your glory, have been shown to us in the simplicity of a child. Our eyes have been opened. As we walk on the pathway of a new year, a new century, and a new millennium, may we pass on the light, may we bring hope, as we reflect the extraordinary story of 'God with us', of the Word made flesh.

May we never turn our faces from those who are forgotten and who suffer. May we always be a part of a community that makes you and your values a reality, and thereby brings light and hope into our world. In the name of Jesus, the babe, the message and the glory of Bethlehem. Amen

ACKNOWLEDGMENTS

We would like to thank all those who have given us permission to include quotations in this book, as indicated in the list below. Every effort has been made to trace and acknowledge copyright holders of all the quotations included in this book. We apologize for any errors or omissions that may remain, and would ask those concerned to contact the publishers, who will ensure that full acknowledgment is made in the future.

'Terrorist' by Jonny Baker and Jon Birch, Proost Publishing, copyright © 1998. Extract from 'Christmas' by John Betjeman, from *Collected Poems*, published by John Murray (Publishers) Ltd. Dietrich Bonhoeffer, from *The Mystery of Holy Night*, copyright © 1996. Used with permission of the Crossroad Publishing Company. Dietrich Bonhoeffer, from *Werke Vol 9, London 1933–1935*, copyright © 1994. Used with permission of the Crossroad Publishing Company. Extract from *A Passion for Life* by Joan Chittister with Icons by Robert Lentz. Text copyright © 1996 by Joan Chittister, OSB. Published in 1996 by Orbis Books, Maryknoll, New York. Alfed Delp, from *The Prison Meditations of Father Delp*, copyright © 1968. Used with permission of the Crossroad Publishing Company. Extract from 'Nothing but a Child', words and music by Steve Earle. Copyright © 1992 Duke of Earle and WB Music Corp, Warner/Chappell Music Limited, London W6 8BS. Reproduced by permission of International Music Publications Ltd. Marian Wright Edelman, 'God, please stop injustice...' from *Guide My Feet*, Beacon Press. Reprinted by the permission of Russell & Volkening as agents for the author. Copyright © 1995 by Marian Wright Edelman. Najwa Farah, *A Continent Called Palestine* (SPCK). 'God our Father, you spoke to the prophets...' copyright © St Georges, Oakdale. Tony Graham, *With Sure Fierce Love Towards Galilee*, copyright © 1998. John Johansen-Berg, 'You teach me to listen' appeared first in *Seeing Christ in Others*, published by SCM-Canterbury Press. 'Come humbly, holy child...' used by permission of The Mothers' Union. Christmas intercession 'Father, in this holy night...' copyright © The Very Revd Michael Perham. 'O God, hear my prayer...' from *The Dreams of My People*, Rima Nasir Tarazi. Extracts from the *Iona Community Worship Book* and *Cloth for the Cradle* (Wild Goose Publications) copyright © Iona Community, Glasgow G51 3UU, Scotland. Extracts from *The Alternative Service Book 1980* and *The Promise of His Glory* are copyright © The Archbishops' Council and are reproduced by permission.